Veronica,
I hope you
enjoy my first
published work!
Best,
Aaron

THE
ADVANTAGE
OF
REAL ESTATE

THE
ADV**A**NTAGE
OF
REAL ESTATE

from Leading Real Estate Experts

Published by Elevate, Charleston, South Carolina.
Member of Advantage Media Group.

ELEVATE is a registered trademark and the
Elevate colophon is a trademark of Advantage Media Group, Inc.

Printed in the United States of America

ISBN: 978-1-60194-012-4

Library of Congress Control Number: 2007930421

Most Advantage Media Group titles are available at special quantity discounts for bulk purchases for sales promotions, premiums, fundraising, and educational use. Special versions or book excerpts can also be created to fit specific needs.

For more information, please write: Special Markets, Advantage Media Group, P.O. Box 272, Charleston, SC 29402 or call 1.866.775.1696.

Publisher's Note: This book is for educational purposes only and represents the varied viewpoints of a team of authors. Neither the authors nor the publisher offer a guarantee that these ideas, techniques or strategies will produce success. The authors and the publisher shall have neither liability nor responsibility to anyone with respect to loss or damage caused or allegedly caused, directly or indirectly, by information contained this book.

TABLE OF CONTENTS

Why Real Estate?

by PATRICK RIDDLE

Patrick Riddle began his successful career in real estate investment while he was a civil engineering student at Clemson University. At the age of 22, he left college and decided to pursue the business full time. Riddle's company, Palmetto Property Solutions, LLC, buys properties mainly in South Carolina. They are continuing to flourish throughout SC and are expanding into other areas.

Riddle is an expert in short sales, lease options, foreclosures, land trusts, and recruiting private money. He has obtained millions of dollars in cash for his company from private investors. Riddle attributes much of his success to his being an avid reader. He has read over 200 books since he began his business including subjects such as marketing, management, leadership, real estate, accelerated learning, sales, psychology, and personal development. He is a certified Practitioner of Neuro-Linguistic Programming.

Patrick Riddle is 26 years old, single, and resides in Charleston, South Carolina. Being a teacher at heart, he is dedicated to sharing his knowledge and experience with others.

Why Real Estate?

AFTER MY JUNIOR YEAR AT CLEMSON UNIVERSITY, two of my friends and I moved to Charleston, South Carolina, for the summer. We were the guys who were always thinking of ideas of how we were going to make some extra money, but prior to this particular summer, we had never done too much about it.

I always knew I was not going to follow the mold that society demanded: *Go to school, get good grades, get a secure job, and work for someone for the rest of your life.* I knew that there had to be another way; I just didn't have any clue what that might be until one of my friends met a fellow in the yard of one of the houses he owned. The man owned several rental properties, acquired over the past few years, each one earning an average of $200 a month. He also told my friend that whether he worked or not, he was making over a thousand dollars a month from his houses... and this guy was only twenty-seven years old!

When my friend told us about his conversation, we were fired up. We decided the first logical step was to go to Barnes and Noble and buy a couple books about real estate investing.

I had never been much of a reader. The only reason I went to a bookstore was to buy the Cliff Notes on whatever book we were supposed to read for school. I still remember the feeling of walking down the aisle in the bookstore and the excitement of it all. I was astounded at the claims of the titles of some the books.

One of the books we bought was *How to Make Millions in Real Estate in Three Years Starting with No Cash.* Before we bought that book, I had never heard of buying property without any money. It didn't seem possible. How could you buy anything without any money? We had planned to use some of the money we had saved for our first real estate venture. Since we were college students, we decided that if there was a way to buy property without any money, we were determined to figure out how. The other book we bought was *Making Big Money in Real Estate.*

After I opened one the books and began to read something seriously for the first time in my life, I couldn't put it down. **This was it!** This was what I had been looking for. Growing up, I was always good at math and the numbers made sense: Buy a house from someone who "needs" to sell it and pay $70,000 for it. Put a few thousand dollars into repairing the property and getting it into good condition. Then either sell the property for market value at $100,000 for a nice profit, or hold onto the property, put a tenant in it, and hold the property as a strategy to create wealth through appreciation, leveraging, and tax benefits.

APPRECIATION

Historically, real estate values have gone up, but no matter what happens in the market, people have to live somewhere. Yes, there have been housing market crashes and corrections, and there always will be. But as long as you position yourself to hold onto your real estate investments for the long term, the value *will* go up. My caution is this: If you buy investment properties do NOT put yourself in a financial bind. Be sure that you have the financial stability to hold onto your properties and wait out any market downturns.

It is important to treat appreciation in real estate as a long-term benefit, not necessarily as something to depend on to make or break the deal.

When we began our business, one of the properties that we purchased only needed some general cosmetic repairs. We had the carpets cleaned, painted the interior, treated the property for termites, and made a few other miscellaneous repairs. We refinanced the property in order to get a better loan. The property was valued at $105,000. Just fifteen months later, the tenants decided that they wanted to purchase the property and so they ordered a new appraisal. The new appraisal came in at $121,000! In just over a year, the property's value had increased by $16,000— without any additional repairs.

GET INVOLVED

By becoming involved in your local community, you may be able to purchase properties that are likely to appreciate significantly. One possibility is that you can look at your area's ten-year growth projections and buy properties that will put you in the path of progress for upcoming residential and commercial developments. If you find out a big retailer has just purchased some property nearby or that a shopping center has been planned in your area, property in those areas would certainly have good potential for appreciation.

Ray Kroc, the founder of McDonald's, said that his business was real estate. That's a very interesting statement. The first time that I read that, I had trouble wrapping my mind around the idea. McDonald's owns some of the most valuable street corners all over the world. They put a tremendous amount of research into their locations for new restaurants. McDonald's buys as much of the real estate right around their new location as they can because they know that their presence increases the value of all of the land around them. Next time you see a McDonald's and some other fast food chains right beside them, think about the fact that they may be renting from McDonald's.

When Disney was planning to build Walt Disney World, they quietly looked at different spots across the country. When they decided upon Florida for their park, they sent out a team to lock up the property they needed. Their team worked with a number of different property owners to purchase all of the property that Disney currently owns. Several people from Disney put options on the properties in various names so that they would not tip off any local landowners about their plans. (An option is an agreement that ties up a piece of property so that you have a right to purchase it under whatever terms and time period are negotiated.) Disney exercised all of the options simultaneously and was able to buy thousands of acres of property for unbelievable prices. As soon as word leaked out that Disney was coming to Florida, all of the properties that bordered Disney shot up in value. If you can get the inside track on upcoming developments, you stand the chance of making a lot of money on real estate investments.

LEVERAGE

Leverage means using borrowed funds to increase your purchasing power. You may have heard it referred to as OPM, or *Other People's Money*. It doesn't matter what you call it, or whether you borrow it from a bank or from your

Uncle Mike. Borrowed funds can be used to accelerate your wealth and put you on the fast track.

Let's say you want to buy a property for $250,000. If you are using a bank for the financing, you might put $25,000 down and the bank will most likely lend you the other $225,000. If you were to invest that same $25,000 into a mutual fund at a 6% annualized return, you would only have $25,000 working for you. On the other hand, if you bought the house, you would have an asset that is worth $250,000 working for you. Over the past few decades, the average appreciation of real estate has been 6%.

An important point to remember is that equity does not have a rate of return. If you get an equity line to gain access back to the $25,000 investment, you can use the funds for leverage into another house or investment, and the house will still appreciate. In addition, accessing the cash through a loan does not initiate any tax ramifications because that money would be proceeds of a loan.

Our strategy focuses on borrowing money from people as opposed to borrowing money from banks. This has worked well for us because with banks, there can be a lot of red tape and hoops to jump through, fees, and paperwork.

We typically buy properties for around 65-75% of value. We want to borrow enough money to pay for the purchase of the property, repairs, marketing, and holding costs. Banks lend money based on the appraised value or purchase price, whichever is lower. We do not want a loan just for the purchase price. By borrowing from private individuals, we can borrow enough money to do everything needed. Once we have renovated the property and it is in good condition, it is easier to work with banks to get a refinance loan, as opposed to a purchase loan if you want to hold onto the property. Then we can cash out our investors, and everyone is happy.

Financing properties through banks can also take a lot of time. Most of the deals that we structure are very time sensitive, and we have learned that good deals have a short shelf life. If it takes too long to close on a property, you are in danger of losing the deal. When we contract a great deal, we like to close on the property as soon as possible. Often, we can close within a week or two of putting a contract on a piece of property. If we were obtaining loans from banks on these deals that would most likely be impossible. We have developed a list of trusted investors (mostly friends and family). We use cash to purchase a majority of our properties and can close as soon as we verify all of our numbers and know that the title is clear.

RESOURCES

You are probably saying to yourself that you don't know anyone who will loan you enough money to get a deal done. Well, you are about to. A great resource for investors for quick financing are what is called hard money lenders, people who are in the business of lending money to real estate investors based on the property. They are typically not concerned with all of the things that banks care about because they know that in the worst case scenario, they get the property back and then they can make all of the money that the investor could have made. Hard money lenders typically charge between 12-18% interest, a few points (a point is a fee paid to a lender and equals 1% of the loan principal), and give you 6-12 months to pay off the loan. Maybe you think that is too expensive, but how much would it cost you if you lost a deal? If you have other options—good, but when you need to close a deal in less than a week, or if you don't have access to the cash or credit necessary to buy a house, these lenders can be a great resource.

Finding a hard money lender in your area who will work with you will enable you to have the confidence to make cash offers. Often, when a seller is motivated to sell their property fast, they need the money yesterday. They may have had their property listed and it didn't sell; or maybe they are behind on payments and facing foreclosure; or maybe they are getting divorced and they never want to see their ex again, and the only thing left between them is the house.

We have seen them all. There are numerous reasons people want to sell fast, so make it your goal to be in the position to make them a cash offer.

Because of the way that we structured many of our deals, they did not require any cash directly out of our pockets, but they did require cash. Remember, hard moneylenders will lend investors money to buy properties. If you are buying a piece of property at a low enough loan to value, they will loan you the money so that you are able to buy, renovate, and sell the property with no cash out of your pocket. Now *that* is a "No Money Down" deal because it did not require any money from your personal resources.

I am not saying that it is always the best idea not to use your own money, but it definitely opens up more investment possibilities. The first year that we got into investing, we contracted a property in our area for $112,000. It was a great deal for that price and we knew it. The seller had lived there for several years and owned it free and clear. She had some family up north and she wanted to move to be with them; she was ready to pack her bags and leave. (You may be asking why she would sell to us at such at great price but one thing that we make sure to never do is to think for anyone else. That can be one of the most costly mistakes you ever make.) We told this seller that we could close within two weeks and she signed on the dotted line. At that time, we did not have the available cash to buy the property, but we knew that if we showed the deal to enough people, we would find the money. Yes, it was a bold move but we were bold kids right out of college.

Through determination and resolve, we found someone who could give us the financing in time. This person had been in real estate for years, and he recognized a good deal. We cut him in on 25% of the net profit for providing the financing and the deal was done. All that the property needed was around $8,000 in cosmetic repairs. At that time, the market was really hot, and the house sold for full price at $171,000 the day we listed it. From the day we purchased the house to when we had a check in hand, it was right under two months.

Don't get too excited though, most deals take a lot longer to turn into cash than that, especially if you are doing some renovations and marketing the house. Still, this was another great deal that required no cash out of our pocket.

YOU CAN SEE IT, TOUCH IT, AND FEEL IT

Real estate is tangible. You can drive by a piece of property and look at it. You can walk around the property and touch it. If you don't know how to evaluate a property yet, there are professionals who can help. You may already have a friend who is a realtor, contractor, appraiser, or inspector. Any of these people can help you get started. By learning how to evaluate a property yourself or by using professionals, all of the numbers will tell you exactly what you need to know to make an educated investment decision.

If you can walk through a house and evaluate what repairs need to be done and do them yourself, that is a great way to build equity in your investment. If your dad was a handyman and taught you how to do tons of miscellaneous property repairs, you have a leg up on everyone else. The only thing that I knew how to do when we got started was painting, but it came in handy on the first few houses we bought. If you plan to fix up the homes yourself, you can simply exchange your time for money in equity, commonly referred to as "sweat equity." This can save you a lot of money and maybe you will even enjoy doing the work. What a great way to spend your time rather than wasting it in front of the TV!

NOW WHAT?

Real estate investing is not easy. Everyone would quit their jobs and do it if it were. From contracting property, evaluating it, getting it financed, purchased, renovated, leased, managed, or sold—many components have to be put together. If you can afford to use professionals all the way through the process such as realtors, attorneys, contractors, property managers, etc., it can make the process easier.

The best decision we ever made was to become educated first about what we planned to do. We bought books, courses, and attended seminars to learn as much as we could. We had rules in our house for an entire month. No one was allowed to watch TV or listen to music. We forced ourselves to listen to nothing but real estate CDs in our cars. We joined the local real estate investors association. We decided to take action and learn as much from seasoned veterans as we could. Our mentor told us that whenever he got started, the best advice he was ever given was by someone who said: "You can either pay for your education or pay for your mistakes and paying for your mistakes is far more expensive."

We took our mentor's advice and gained twenty-five years experience at that moment. Our mentor had seen everything happen in the market. He prepared us for what was to come. Any time we had questions, we knew where to find answers.

Whether you just want to pick up a few houses to pay for your retirement or whether you want to work as a full-time real estate investor, reading this book is your good start. While you are reading, go out and begin talking to friends, family, or anyone who will talk to you about real estate. Put the word out that you are a real estate investor and that you are looking for a good investment.

Take action and get started. Don't be one of those people who have been reading about investing and going to all the seminars and five years later, still have not bought the first investment property. Don't just educate yourself, but put your knowledge into action!

Contact information & Additional Resources:

To obtain Patrick's free CD, *9 Ways to Profit as a Real Estate Investor in the Next 90 Days*, please visit **www.FreeRealEstateInvestingCD.com**

Patrick's office may be contacted at (843) 849-8991.

CONNECTING YOUR NETWORK TO GROW YOUR NET WORTH

by ROB KONECNY

As REAL ESTATE iNVESTORS, we recognize the power of financial leverage using other people's money or credit. Whether you're investing part-time to supplement your income or are a full time investor, this chapter is designed to help you leverage your time and allow you to keep more of the money you earned, by identifying a key element to your business that most investors over look as they move forward into the realm of investing in real estate. Regardless of your experience, or what your investment strategies are, you are a business owner. As a business owner, you must build a network of the professionals identified in this chapter to leverage your time so you are free to devote more time to growing your business. As you read through this chapter, you will meet the members you need in your network as team players, their roles and the basic service they provide. If you lead them well, your network will increase your net worth. It is now time to meet the players who will either make you money, save you money, or save you time. Rob Konecny is the President of Property Locators, LLC and is responsible for developing a network of Professional Property Locators who locate and research distressed properties for he and his partners to purchase and remodel through American Quest Investments, located in Phoenix Arizona.

CONNECTING YOUR NETWORK TO GROW YOUR NET WORTH

FROM MY EXPERIENCE INVESTING IN RESIDENTIAL REAL ESTATE, I discovered that part of my success can be attributed to building and leading a vast network of individuals who all had a role in helping me grow my business. As an investor, you will want to do the same. So, within your network there will be a nucleus of several team players who you must nurture a relationship with because of the direct financial impact they can have on your business. These professional core members will directly impact every transaction you become involved in. They are the planners and engineers of your business model. As business advisors, their skill and knowledge in acquisitions and sales of properties in your portfolio will significantly impact your wealth building objectives.

The other team members within your network will serve you in a more peripheral manner, particularly after a transaction is completed and you have acquired a property. Typically, these members are the professionals that will serve you in the trades or a management capacity. The focus of this chapter will be on the key players you need within your network who are going to either make or save you money, and how to leverage their expertise to save you time.

When I began my education by reading books and attending seminars on real estate investing, I had heard on several occasions how investing was a team sport. It was further explained that the "do it yourself" types could certainly build their portfolio over time but it was a longer path. The "do it yourself" types lost the ability to leverage other people's time and expertise while building a substantial portfolio. The "do it yourself" types business was cyclical because once their resources of time and money were expended, their ability to grow their business came to a stand still until either more funding or time became available. As an investor, money is not an issue if the deal is great. There are many private sources of money available that will lend against property. My objective in writing this chapter is helping you become more familiar with the concept of leveraging other people's time to grow your business. Failing to become a leveraged investor, using the time, expertise, and skills of those in your network, at some point will certainly cost you money. You will invariably miss out on investment opportunities and additional savings by failing to build a solid team around you and your business.

As a young boy, my first exposure to leadership and team building was the Cub Scouts. Later I advanced to the Boy Scouts, becoming an Eagle Scout. During those formative years, Mom and Dad's were obviously the leaders, telling the scouts what to do and when to do it. The expectations of the meeting or activity were set and we scouts performed. As a young scout, it became very clear that, even though the adults were in charge, a hierarchical peer level of leaders existed. Within the pack or troop, those that assumed responsibility and helped out where needed, were often recognized by our parents. Our leaders mentored those fledgling leaders and we became the "go to kids," the teenagers that could get things done within our peer group. We were the ones the adults would count on to share instructions and directions with our peers. Whether it was an activity or a chore, the instructions and assignments were passed down and shared collectively by our group either together or individually, in order to achieve a desired outcome for the pack or troop.

As I grew older and began to participate in various team sports, the concept of leadership and teams continued to expand and I began to understand the power of leverage for the greater good of the team. It started with a Coach, teaching and defining each team member's role and function. The Coach relied on the Team Captain to direct the players and set the plays in motion. The players then executed their assigned role during the play, moving the team forward toward the goal of winning the game. If a team wasn't winning, it was time to change. That change could be a different strategy, different execution, additional practice, or in some instances a player rotation as a reminder to the players by the coach that there is no "I" in team. A win was attributed to the collective efforts of the team members.

As I was promoted through the ranks in the US Army, the early lessons on leadership, team building, communication, and collectively leveraging the efforts of others in the chain of command were driven home time and again. Generals would define the goals, communicate through Senior

Officers and Non-Commissioned Officers, missions and orders, down to the Regiment, Division, and Battalion level. Based on mission requirement, the tasks assignments would then be broken down even further to Company, Platoon and Squad Levels; finally to individual soldiers who followed those orders for the completion of the overall mission. Talk about a logistical challenge. Law enforcement agencies across the country still follow the same military style chain of command in order to maintain safer communities and to keep continuity within the organization. Fortunately, as a real estate investor, your logistical requirement will not be so daunting.

Before you can actually begin building your team and creating your investors network, you have a few in-house tasks to perform if you want your team to maximize your investment effort. As Team Captain, if you want to create leverage you must clearly define your business plan, your goals and your objectives. What will be your investment niche—residential, commercial, or land? What are your short and long term goals? What resources do you have available? What resources do you need? Who has or can bring the additional resources, expertise or skill you will need to grow your business. While reading this chapter, I suggest you keep a notebook and pen handy so you may begin forming your team or adding to your existing team. You may have already started building your team but have identified a gap that needs to be filled in your business model that you can now seek out to create additional leverage. Don't just highlight it, but take the time to write yourself a note so you won't forget to fill the gap.

I was just five short years away from Retirement from my law enforcement career, when I caught the real estate investing bug. One of the most fortunate breaks I had starting out, was meeting, befriending, and finally partnering with several very successful multi- million dollar real estate investors. I knew I wanted to be where they were and was willing to pay a price to learn what they knew. It was a quid pro quo, they got coffee, lunch, dinner and an occasional cigar, and I got to pick their brains for the knowledge and experience they were willing to share.

The point is that you need to seek out, find, and nurture these gems as friends. By surrounding yourself with those worthy of being a role model to learn from, you will accelerate your business by duplicating that which successfully has already been done by those you are seeking to model after. This inner circle of new found friends will provide you counsel, insight, and guidance based on their experience. They may have no vested financial interest in your business; however, I have found time and again their interest really lies in seeing you succeed financially. They are your sounding board, a safety net, an inside source whose connections within their own network could help you with your business.

My point is for you go out and find a mentor who has been down the road you want to travel. Do not seek counsel from those who are not where you want to be. Though often well meaning, their counsel will only serve as a negative reinforcement of everything that can possibly go wrong because they don't know any better. If they have not experienced or done what you have set out to accomplish, realistically what can you expect to learn?

Upon proving you are deserving of their time, successful investors are always willing to help, because they realize helping you achieve what you want in the end helps them achieve what they want. You will come to find that successful people believe in paying it forward. Because real estate investors are almost a community within a community, sharing a common bond and socializing within the same spheres of influence, they are not difficult to find. You want to build an inner council of those whose wisdom and experience exceeds your own skills and talent. To grow your business, you do not want to be the smartest person in the room. Join a real estate club or investment club. After attending a couple of meetings you should have identified who the players are. Introduce yourself or asked to be introduced. A great way to start the relationship after the introduction is simply ask what you might be able to do to help their business or the organization while you are building your business.

To have my questions answered, some of the best nuggets of advice were often gleaned informally by arriving at a meeting or workshop early and helping set up for the event. Not only did I get noticed, but also this practice opened the door to even more informal question/answer sessions while staying afterwards to help clean up. Quid Pro Quo! As you build your relationships, you will be amazed how much you can learn by just springing for a coffee or meal.

Now that you have established your business model, begin to build relationships outside your everyday sphere of influence, it is time to identify who else should be on your support team and why. As team captain, leadership, communications and execution begins with you. You must clearly share and communicate your vision with each team member defining what your expectations are and verifying what they can or cannot do for you. You need to be very specific, painting a vivid and complete picture for them to be able to identify with your objective. Once your goals are known they can then formulate their role in just how they are able to help you accomplishing your goal and reach your objective.

Visually picture and see your business as a spoked wheel from the old western covered wagons and stagecoaches. You and your trusted council of mentors are the axel centered within the axel hub. The hub is formed with the skilled professionals that allow the axel to turn and keep your business moving. These team members will be directly involved from start to finish any transaction you and your business are a part of. From the axel hub connecting to the wheel are spokes to provide shape and strength to the wheel. Think of these spokes as team members whose role is to provide strength and shape to your business wheel. The more spokes you have for support the stronger and more durable the wheel becomes in handling the terrain. Consider these spokes, as team members needed to support your business wheel providing strength and durability. Though they are peripheral in nature, they will still have contact with your investments, and providing you service, but in a much more limited manner.

In a team sport analogy, these team members may act as either an offensive or defensive player for your real estate business. These are the professional team members looking out for your best interest and allowing you to further leverage your time and resources. Remember you want to work on growing your business, not spending valuable time working in your business.

Most investors, especially new ones, tend to believe the first team member they need to establish a relationship is a Realtor. I disagree; if you are investing in real estate, you are a business owner. As a business owner, I believe you should immediately seek the advice and services of a certified public accountant as well as a financial planner. It is imperative that your accountant and financial planner are real estate investment oriented. Your accountant and financial planner are worth their weight in gold. As players, your accountant and financial planner have both offensive and defensive roles to execute in your business. They are front-line players and the first team members within your business that will make you money, save you money, or keep you out of trouble with the Internal Revenue Service.

Offensively, your CPA will be able to advise you on deductions, tax strategies, and a number of variations all legal and benefiting you as a business owner. Defensively they are your closet ally should you be audited by the Internal Revenue Service.

Your real estate financial planner is an offensive team player, though most would think they would be defensive in nature. Here is why I see a financial planner as an offensive player. Setting up your business using the proper entities is an offensive strategy, that when structured right, defends your business. The financial planner's role is asset protection, estate planning, and establishing the right entities for your business to operate and grow under.

Because your business entities and accounting practices are closely intertwined, if possible make your first or second meeting a joint meeting between your CPA and Financial Planner. This joint meeting allows them the opportunity to dialogue directly with you and each other regarding what the best pathways are for you immediately and in the future as your business grows and expands. You will also learn what they expect from you as a client. For services rendered, expect to be billed by the hour, and in some instances a simple flat fee, by both your CPA and financial planner. If your financial planner doesn't bill by the hour or wants to move you into investing outside of real estate, find a new planner.

Your next team player should be a real estate attorney. Your real estate attorney's primary role is defense. His counsel and expertise are designed to protect you and your interests. Whether your state requires real estate closings take place through attorneys or you live in a state where closings take place through a title company you will want a competent real estate attorney on your team.

A good real estate attorney can structure and review your contracts and purchase offers, leases, rental agreements, and be a significant help in legally structuring transactions that involve creative financing during much larger transactions. Your attorney should also be well versed in the landlord–tenant laws or acts covered in federal, state and community levels. Your attorney will be able to assist you at court proceedings, evictions and claims of restitution.

If you have any questions or concerns regarding a transaction, do not hesitate to contact your attorney for clarification or review before signing a binding contract you are unfamiliar with. It is better to delay the transaction, for your attorney's review, until you are clear about what you are agreeing to in a contract. A review by your attorney upfront is less costly than having to pay a small fortune to your attorney trying to undo your mistake and hoping it doesn't cost you even more money. Don't operate your business on the pay later principal. It doesn't work and there are many real estate investors who have either paid dearly for their education or been put out of business via the school of litigation.

From a financial perspective, ending up in litigation is not a win-win scenario. If an agreement is reached and settled before going to a trial both parties generally walk away feeling jilted. If the litigation actually does go to trial, one party will win and the party will lose. The only true winner in either of these scenarios will be the litigating attorney's. They will get paid regardless of the outcome.

I can't put too much emphasis on the need to have a competent CPA, financial planner, and attorney who all specialize in real estate on your team. They are there to assist you as the need arises. The money you invest up front for their services will be recouped in no time, either as savings, credits, de-ductions or minimizing law suits and litigation expense from future sellers, buyers and tenants. The bottom line is on your balance sheet. Investing and building your relationships within these professional team players will allow you to maximize your profits and keep more of the money you have earned.

If you live in a state were real estate transaction are completed through a Title Company, you will want to build a long term relationship with a title agent working for a Title Company that is real estate investor oriented. Truth be told, Investors are a lot of work because often we are non-traditional buyers or sellers when it comes to creatively structuring and financing our deals. Investor purchases are often outside the box of the typical conventional process used by the average homebuyer.

Make sure your title agent and their company understands investors, the creative structuring of deals involving entities, joint venturing, partnering and creative financing for non-traditional purchases of a property.

When closing on a transaction, your title agent role is neutral. They are responsible for ensuring both buyer and sellers have not only met but fulfill the obligations stated in the purchase and sales agreement contract, the dispersal of funds and the recording of the properties transfer of ownership.

From a team perspective, as a buyer, your title agent's role is defensive in nature. Prior to closing, it is their responsibility to ensure you are able to take ownership with a clear title and warranty deed. Public record searches are done on your behalf and if any issues arise that would have a negative impact on the purchase of the property you will be advised. With the information obtained from your title agent, you may either move forward with the transaction or re-evaluate the deal if title is clouded for possibly restructuring the deal or cancellation if title cannot be cleared.

As a seller, your title agent's offensive role is ensuring that the buyer funds are available and ready to disburse at the closing when title is clear and warrantable.

One, of the great things about establishing your relationship with a title agent are some additional time saving resources they often offer as freebies or at a very minimal cost. As investors who are constantly buying or selling properties, even though we create an enormous amount of work, we are repeat business for the title company.

The first incentive I encourage to ask for, are investor rates for the services they provide in a closing. The fee's you would normally pay as a typical homebuyer doing a conventional purchase will be substantially reduced as an enticement for repeat business. In addition, Title companies often have a data service for comparables and foreclosure listings that they will allow you to access for free or for a very minimal service charge. Title companies also offer to do advertisements and bulk mailing for you for a nominal charge. Again you are looking for ways to leverage your time. You may pay a small fee but it is certainly worth the leverage it creates for you by allowing them to help with your marketing and advertisement so you can continue looking for deals that generate an increase in revenue. If you don't want to physically go to the Title Company office to open escrow or attend the closing, use the title company's courier service, again a minimal charge. Take advantage of these different services to leverage your time. Not only will it make things more convenient but allows to maximize and make better use of your time as an investor.

Now that you have established your business and legal team of professionals to assist you in establishing, protecting and keeping more of the money you earn in your business, let's look at finding a Realtor and adding them to your team.

Many new residential real estate investors are taught that they need to immediately start working with a Realtor. Realtors in general maintain this mystical persona of holding some magical key to the "Great Deal Kingdom" and only they are capable of finding you a "great deal." If you are focusing on residential real estate investments, do you need a Realtor on your team? Yes but probably not for the reasons commonly thought of.

Before I explain what you need and do not need a Realtor for, understand I am not picking on Realtors. My wife and several of our friends are Realtors and are very successful in their profession. First, you must understand a Realtor's role and why you should not expect to find many great deals through a realtor. A realtor's profession is sales. They are professional sales people whose income is generated in the form of a commission based on a percentage of the sales price. Their professional business role is selling land, residential, and commercial properties. Their function is to bring buyers and sellers together, and broker through price and terms a purchase and sales transaction of the aforementioned real estate investments that are not only agreeable to the seller and buyer, but deemed to be representative of their fiduciary responsibilities to the best interest of their clients. Upon the closing of a successful transaction the commission is then split between the two agents, unless negotiated otherwise.

If you understand this, then you understand that when you are looking to purchase residential real estate for investment purposes, a vast majority of realtors are not likely to find you the types of discounted properties you are looking to purchase. In addition, the Realtors purchase and sales agreement by and large is not investor friendly. Refer back to our discussion regarding your real estate attorney preparing your contracts. You want to have a specific verbiage in both your purchase and sales contracts that are very specific in protecting your interests. By and large properties listed on the Multiple Listing Service are a waste of your time. The seller is looking for a retail buyer. The tried and true investor is looking for at least a thirty percent discount in order to realize a profit if flipping a property. If you are looking at buy and hold rental property no less than twenty if not a twenty-five percent discount provided the property is less than five years old and very clean. Do not become a speculator of appreciation when making a purchase decision. Get out on the street to find and negotiate your own deals.

So when should use a Realtor? A Realtor can provide you with information to help you evaluate what a property is worth based on the active listings, pending sales, and homes that have sold in the area of a home you may be considering for a purchase. While there are other resources available for doing comparables, the realtors are on the street and generally in the know regarding current market conditions. Remember in the majority of Realtor's vocabulary, the words "price reduced" equates to a good deal. I don't know that it has ever been said, but personally I have yet to see a Realtor's advertisement or listing state "discounted thirty percent below market value."

While looking at investment properties to purchase, a Realtor can provide you a comparative market analysis, a valuable tool in evaluating what your maximum target purchase price should be. While building the relationship with a realtor respect their time. A realtor's time is just as valuable as yours. Let them know up front that by helping you now in the future when you have a property to sell, you will let them have the listing. Selling a property is where your Realtor is worth every bit of their commission.

Remember they are professional sales people. Leverage your time and let them do their job of selling your property for the highest price possible. Yes you can attempt to sell the house on your own to save a few bucks, but go back to what your time is worth. Do you want to spend your time marketing, advertising and holding open houses, dealing with buyers and all their questions; or should you let the Realtor deal with it so you spend your time looking for more deals. Use the services of a Realtor when you are selling a property is a great way to leverage your time.

So how do you find a good Realtor to begin building a relationship with? First you will want to find a Realtor who is investor savvy, however remember if they are investor savvy they are looking for good deals that are deeply discounted. Here is tip taught to me by my partners as I was starting out. If you meet a Realtor, let them know you are an investor and you would like them to send you their one best deal. If they immediately start asking about what you are looking for, or what your parameters are, you have just met a Realtor who is going to try and swamp your e-mail with every listing they can find to send to you. An investor savvy Realtor will know that you are looking to find and purchase discounted investment properties and will occasionally send you something that is worth a look and may occasionally make the grade as a possible investment property. If it turns out to be a property that you would purchase, use the agent to make the offer and let them earn the commission, after all they created the opportunity for you so let them be compensated accordingly.

Upon identifying a residential property as an investment, and placing it under a contract, you now begin your due diligence during the inspection period. During the inspection period, you may or may not need the services of a property inspector and or an appraiser to help you justify your purchase price or negotiate the contract. Both the inspector and an appraiser will provide you with information needed to make a calculated purchase that will be profitable.

If the home is than less than five years old, I would not concern myself with a property inspection unless I visually noted some thing that would cause me to believe the building was structurally unsound. Since newer homes are still under warranty, problems can be corrected by the builder. Do insist on the termite and organism report. For a home that is five to ten years old, I would consider having the systems inspected. Again these items maybe covered under warranty and can be corrected. Anything over ten years old would be subject to a complete inspection. Things break down and wear out and if I am purchasing a property I want to now what unseen additional costs I might be facing when considering my purchase price.

To determine the market value of a property most investors rely on comparables obtained from a Realtor. The lenders in order to minimize their risk on a loan against a property, primarily use an appraisal. The appraisal is an apples to apples comparison of similar homes in a geographical area to determine the value of a property. Depending on market conditions, an appraisal can be used as a guideline when placing offers on properties

Keep in mind that an appraisal simply compares apples to apples when establishing a value to a property. A seller will often use the appraised price to justify their asking sales price. Keep in mind that current market conditions should dictate how you view the appraisal when compared to a sales price.

Here is an example of when you may want to order your own appraisal of a property. Let's say you have found a property that you intend to rehab. You had the property inspected and the property has some issues that were identified and will need to be fixed. During the inspection you have decided to move some walls to open up the home, and do an addition to the existing structure. An appraisal can be used to determine if the money you are going to spend on the renovations can be justified against the after-repair value of the property by a lender. Putting too much money into a rehab property that a conventional lender won't loan against is simply a headache you do not want. Don't speculate on how much the value of a property will increase if you remodel or renovate other than what you can conceive of. The numbers never lie.

Your financial wealth as a real estate investor is the bottom line. Nobody should care about this more than you. However, as an investor it is up to you to go out and not only build, maintain, and lead your team members that have been identified for you but to build nurturing relationships. Lunches, cards, simple remembrances, and invitations to social gatherings can go a long way. Respect their time and engage them as needed and they will make and save you money, and leverage your time. They are worth their weight in gold, apply the golden rule and treat them accordingly. Prosperous Investing!!

Contact information & Additional Resources:

To learn more about their investment companies and investment opportunities visit the company website: **www.propertylocatorsite.com**

or contact Rob by email: **Rob@propertylocatorsite.com**.

Finding
Motivated Sellers

by DARON CAMPBELL

DARON CAMPBELL is MANAGING PARTNER of RE/MAX Commercial Real Estate, based in Sherman Oaks, California. RE/MAX Commercial specializes in the sale of apartment buildings, shopping centers and office buildings. As Managing Partner, Mr. Campbell is responsible for the growth and development of the company and for increasing its profitability. Under Mr. Campbell's leadership, RE/MAX Commercial has been named by the Los Angeles Business Journal as the fastest growing commercial real estate company in California for four consecutive years with 2005 sales volume exceeding $1.2 billion. In addition to managing the company's 71 commercial associates, Mr. Campbell is the President of RE/MAX Commercial's Apartment Sales Group, which specializes in the sale of apartment complexes in Southern California. With over $1 billion in personal career sales, Daron Campbell ranks among the elite of the most active and successful realtors in the United States. He has been recognized in each of his 6 years with RE/MAX as one of the top 1% of all real state agents in the United States. He was recently given the RE/MAX Lifetime Achievement Award and inducted into the RE/MAX Hall of Fame, achieving that plateau in record time. He was also named the #1 RE/MAX Agent in the State of California out of 11,000 agents for 2005.

Finding Motivated Sellers

THE GREATEST OF ALL SUCCESSFUL REAL ESTATE INVESTORS all believe in one principle: "You make money in real estate when you buy not when you sell." This driving principle is a concept that fuels the desire in people to make the great deal going into a transaction and ensures the most favorable result whenever they choose to sell. In the quest to find the best opportunities in real estate to buy, it is important to be clear where to go to source those opportunities on a consistent basis. Whether you are a realtor or an investor, the objective is the same; Find the shortest route to a closed transaction that all parties involved are incentivized to complete. The greatest opportunities for both the realtor and the investor are to locate a seller who is motivated to consummate a deal.

How is it that certain property listings sell in twenty-four hours or less with multiple offers, while others languish and grow stale for months leaving both agent and seller tense, embarrassed and disappointed? How often are agents ashamed to make contact with the seller because the only news to report is "There's been no new activity?" The primary difference between the properties that sell quickly and those that do not is that properties which sell quickly tend to do so because they have a motivated seller. The ease with which an agent lists, sells, and closes a listing with a motivated seller, versus that of one with an unmotivated seller is about as extreme as one can imagine. In fact, the distance between these two polar opposites is also the quantifying factor which separates the overwhelmingly successful real estate agents from the rest of the pack. The agents at the top of the brokerage "food chain" focus most of their time, energy and marketing, on identifying motivated sellers. These elite few realize that their precious time is most effectively spent working hard to find the easy transactions. And the easiest of all transactions by far, are those with motivated sellers.

The savviest of investors also focus their investment strategies around the search for sellers of properties which offer unique or special opportunities for profit due largely to the particular motivation of the seller. The "buy low" opportunities in any given market are the result of a seller realizing a need to "get out now" even if it means selling for less than the market dictates or selling at a loss.

The more motivated a seller tends to be, the more likely it is that a transaction will be completed. The main difference between a motivated seller and an un-motivated seller is one simple thing;

A motivated seller has a particular reason they need to sell as opposed to just wanting to sell and will do whatever necessary to facilitate a closed escrow on their property.

This difference can mean millions of dollars in the pockets of a knowledgeable realtor or an astute investor if they know what to look for and never compromise their objectives.

WHAT CHARACTERIZES A MOTIVATED SELLER?

How does one identify a motivated seller? What are the particular signals that indicate motivation? And who are the "insiders" who can point out motivated sellers to us? The answers to these questions are the keys to unlock the real estate riches awaiting any agent or investor who is willing to invest a little time and energy into finding them in a given market.

First, a motivated seller is one whose determination to sell and move on is greater than his need to capture the last dollar. This seller is interested in securing a legitimate buyer who can assure a closed escrow within a certain time frame. The motivated seller will trade real dollars (sometimes thousands and thousands of dollars) in exchange for that assurance. So initially, the first indication of a motivated seller is pricing. If you know your marketplace and are familiar with your product type, you should be well aware of pricing trends as well as being aware of the recent sales comparables. When you find a seller who is willing to price a property at or below the price of the lowest comparable sale, you have a strong indication of a seller who is "ready to deal".

From the realtor's point of view, it is of paramount importance to illustrate the range of the recent sales comparables and for a fast sale, recommend similar pricing to that of the lowest legitimate comparable. Motivated sellers are much more amenable to "accurate" market pricing than are sellers without any particular motivation. A seller with a reason to sell will listen to logic and will respond favorably to pricing recommendations when presented with proper supporting evidence. They are not interested in "testing" the market with a price that both seller and realtor know is too high. Nor are they prone to want to try new pricing gimmicks like "value range pricing" or "unpriced" listings which are open for bid. These tactics are readily utilized by sellers who are in no particular hurry or have an unrealistic viewpoint regarding the value of their property. These are the listings which sit on the market for weeks and months with no offers. The expert listing agent has little time for this type of seller because he knows that he may spend many valuable hours and significant marketing dollars on a listing that is not likely to sell any time soon.

Who are these mysterious sellers who are seemingly willing to forego thousands of dollars in order to consummate a sale? They are, in a word, everywhere! Motivated sellers aren't born; they are created by life's circumstances. Think about the many curves life can throw that might create a motivated seller: death, divorce, taxes, partnership dissolution, natural disasters, failed businesses and foreclosures just to name a few. Each of these scenarios is likely to incite the need to shuffle assets and make financial adjustments for the people involved. Each seller in these instances typically has a need to sell rather than a simple desire to sell. The mitigating circumstances caused by their plight, many times force the sale of some of or all of the assets involved. This spells opportunity for the clever realtor who can find the seller and the investor who can seize the opportunity.

So how do we uncover motivation? When dealing directly with a seller, the level of motivation may not be obvious or spoken of in an effort by the seller to avoid seeming desperate. As a result, the expert realtor or savvy investor many times must "ferret" out the information which indicates the level of motivation. In these instances, the ability to ask tough questions will be the key. It is essential that we inquire about the seller's wants, needs, timeframes and plans for the proceeds as well as the details about any existing debt, third party liens or any other types of encumbrances. It is also imperative that we determine if there is any distress involved in the scenario. Distress manifests itself in the form of notes coming due, notices of default or trustee sale, court ordered sale and defaulted or delinquent property taxes to name a few. Much of this data can be obtained from the public records. However, if we are fortunate enough to have a direct audience with the seller, it's easier to be told all of the issues by the seller himself.

What are other sources for motivated sellers? There are many resources we are able to utilize to assist us in the identification of motivated sellers. I have sources of properties from each of the following:

Accountants and Financial Planners

The people who handle other people's money are prime candidates to be enlisted as teammates in our quest to find motivated sellers. They are consistently aware of the financial needs of their various clients at any given time. They also tend to be amongst the most trusted advisors for people in all walks of life. Having a number of these financial professionals on your referral team will invariably result in opportunities. A realtor might offer complimentary opinions of value for any client of the accountant or financial planner (sometimes needed during estate planning) in exchange for referrals when a sale is desired or needed.

Title Insurance Companies

Title insurance representatives happen to be a phenomenal resource in the effort to identify motivated sellers. These individuals are privy to many situations and significant amounts of information regarding properties, owners, lien holders and debt information. Property profiles provided by title companies identify all matters which affect the title of a property. As a result, an informed title insurance representative is able to inform us of all existing loan information including those which may be due or are in default, delinquent tax information, third party liens such as mechanics liens which are "clouds" on the title and prevent the owner from selling without clearing. Information about issues such as these may be a resounding signal of seller motivation or even desperation.

Attorneys

Attorneys are another great source for identifying motivated sellers. Attorneys are the facilitators of divorces, probate matters, estate sales, tax resolution and partnership dissolutions among many other things. As a result, they can provide a steady stream of referrals of motivated sellers.

Foreclosure Notification Services

There are many ways to acquire information about properties which have gone into default or are heading toward a trustee sale. These resources range from financial newspapers which publish these notices daily or weekly, to actual foreclosure notification services which will identify such properties and provide pertinent data about the foreclosure. This type of information is invaluable because it identifies situations where extreme motivation is likely to exist. An owner who is in jeopardy of losing a property to foreclosure, many times is prepared to sell quickly and will often settle for little or no money in their own pocket at the closing to gain relief from their current debt. The outstanding debt many times is significantly lower than the value of the home.

Expired Listings

Each day literally thousands of listings expire for properties which have been for sale for a period of time. These expired listings are indicators of a few things; first, we have an owner who, at least at some point, has expressed an interest in selling; secondly, their property did not sell for whatever reason; and third, they have, in all likelihood been disappointed in the marketing process of their property. These owners, many times are primed for an astute investor or a savvy realtor to seize an opportunity that has occurred out of a potential sellers frustration. Many times, this potential seller is now ready to agree to major price concessions sometimes incredibly favorable terms. Information of properties with expired listings may be found in local multiple listing services or obtained from realtors. Many investors hold on to older for sale ads or real estate sections of the newspaper and monitor the status of certain properties over time. Once a few months go by and the property has yet to be sold, they move in with aggressive offers hoping to find a frustrated seller who is pleased to have any interest shown in their property. Many times a spectacular bargain will result.

Bank Real Estate Owned Departments

Once a bank forecloses on a property, the bank becomes the owner of the real estate. Banks tend to be among the most motivated sellers of all. Bad loans which result in foreclosures are a very painful topic at most banking institutions. Put simply, foreclosures are viewed as negative assets by banks and result in certain limits being placed on the banks ability to make other loans. As a result, most banks are extremely anxious to "unload" foreclosed properties or defaulted loans before foreclosure. The bank has a department called the Real Estate Owned department in which asset managers dispose of bad loans and foreclosed properties every day. These asset managers can be the source of spectacular opportunities because their priority is on the disposal of the asset, not the final price of the asset. Therefore, many times a bank will sell property at a steep discount in return for a rapid transaction. Identifying and establishing a relationship with several bank asset managers can be an extremely profitable exercise.

Relocation Departments/Human Resources

One seldom utilized resource for finding motivated sellers is the Human Resource/Relocation department at major companies. The people in this department are in charge of assisting employees with everything associated with relocating to a different branch of the company, including the sale of their home. What better resource for accessing a motivated seller than the people actually facilitating the move? And how much more motivated a seller can there be than one who is definitely moving out of the area within a defined period of time?

Rental Services

An extremely valuable source for finding motivated sellers that is often overlooked is property rental and leasing services. These services provide lists of homes for rent or lease. Typically, this indicates a vacant or soon to be vacant property. Often times, the most motivated sellers are people who are owners of rental properties which are not rented. This is typical because there is usually a mortgage associated with the property and when the property is vacant, the owner must pay that mortgage from their own pocket without the assistance of a tenant. Sometimes that owner will sell at an extremely attractive price to avoid the pain of having to make the mortgage payment out of their own pocket.

These are only some of the many overlooked resources which are available to help find motivated sellers. The key is to use specific strategies and resources such as these to locate people who have a distinct need to sell. Focus on finding those sellers and phenomenal deal-making opportunities will be yours.

Your Approach

The final key to finding and closing motivated sellers is to consciously raise your probabilities of doing business with someone by carefully crafting what you say and how you say it.

Maybe the most critical factor in determining how much success you achieve with potential sellers is your approach or the style in which you convey your desire to be of assistance. How you deliver your message influences the seller's perception of the value you will bring in helping them attempt to accomplish their goals. Ask direct, precise questions. Listen with intensity; it enhances the perception of your intelligence. Never be afraid to ask the difficult questions and demand details. Do your homework and assume the role of an expert. Remember, dominance creates submissiveness. The most knowledgeable people in real estate know the market, know their facts and speak confidently in a very authoritative manner. Don't be afraid to push and ask for what you want. Practice your approach beforehand so that you can deliver your message with the style, charisma, emotion, sharpness and clarity that affects people. Sellers are looking for powerful authorities to help them accomplish their goals and protect their interests. They want guidance! Anticipate any potential objections and handle them before they come up. Also, listen carefully to all objections to determine what the real objection is and what the fear is that lies beneath the resistance.

If at the end of the day you can answer the following questions, you will have unlocked the keys to earn the cooperation of the seller. What is important to the seller about selling? Why is that critical to him/her? How can my involvement be perceived by them as critical to the successful achievement of their objective?

Remember, the objective is to help this seller get what they want and as a result, get what you want. Do not spend excessive amounts of time talking about yourself and how great you are. It is critical to be cognizant of the fact that people are inherently selfish. The most important problem in the world to them is their problem and the most important person in the world to them is them. The greatest of all business minds realize this truth and use their skills adroitly to show empathy and focus on the plight of the other person.

When using any of the previously mentioned methods or resources for finding motivated sellers, you must also incorporate swift, decision-making in the process of assessing whether you have a potential deal or not. If you want to enjoy a high level of success and make tons of money, you must set standards for which kinds of clients with whom you will work and under what circumstances. The purpose of being very specific about these standards is because it is essential to determine a seller's needs, wants, timeframe, financial situation, temperament, sincerity and finally, whether we want to work with this person given each of these. If they don't meet all of your qualifications, don't work with them! Trust your instincts.

QUALifyiNq PROSpECTS

by DORIS HOUCK

DORIS HOUCK, REAlTOR®, HAS bEEN pRACTiCiNq residential and commercial real estate in the Central Florida area since 1985. In 1994, Doris expanded her real estate horizons and established PRISM Partners, Realtors®, where she currently is broker-owner of the independent real estate practice located in Winter Park, Florida. Her consultative sales style provides a knowledgeable and professional approach to the real estate process offering nearly 22 years of sales and marketing experience to insure that the entire buying or selling process is as comfortable as possible. Thanks to a personal network of satisfied clients, friends, family, and professional associates, Doris Houck will continue to enjoy the success that comes from providing excellence in real estate services for this ever-expanding sphere of clients and customers for many years to come. This service begins now as it did when Houck started her real estate career nearly 22 years ago, by qualifying the customer in order to be able to provide a complete package of professional real estate services to match all real estate needs. Doris lives in Winter Park, Florida with her husband of 33 years.

Qualifying Prospects

Effective qualifying can make the dream of selling real estate come true, while having fun & make money at the same time.

What does it mean to qualify prospects? Qualifying is important from several perspectives. During the course of this chapter, and based on my twenty plus years of real estate experience, I will explore the various aspects associated with qualifying that, I trust, will be the most beneficial to both agents and clients alike as you proceed through the buying or selling process. Further, it has been my experience—and as I train the agents that I recruit for my real estate practice—the real estate transaction can be fun and financially rewarding; however, I don't believe it is only about the money. Whether my client is a first-time homebuyer or savvy commercial investor, I start each prospective transaction with the same basic philosophy. We will explore my consultative approach to the real estate transaction in this chapter during the discussion of the various important aspects associated with qualifying.

Qualifying prospective clients is important on several levels. I believe qualifying clients is the most important aspect of my ability to provide the utmost in customer service while maintaining disciplined time management. To demonstrate the usefulness of the practice of qualifying, I would like to provide a scenario of a day-in-my-life and trust that you will find it useful to incorporate into your own qualifying style.

First, let me say, that it is important for either a real estate practitioner or a consumer to be both aware and informed of the various steps involved in a real estate transaction. Initially, the first step in qualifying, also called pre-qualifying, is to determine the purchasing power of the client. In my practice, pre-qualifying is as painless as establishing rapport on the phone, setting an initial appointment, and determining what, if any, real estate service can be provided. Therefore, I believe that consumers should be somewhat familiar with loan programs, interest rates, and their credit picture as they begin their real estate adventure. As a real estate broker, I have long-standing relationships with mortgage bankers, real estate attorneys, and I am up to date on changing laws and concerns associated with zoning, construction, termites, and more. Although my practice is real estate, I need to be aware of the potential concerns that a buyer or seller may have so that I can direct them in the proper direction as the transaction proceeds. However, the first step is qualifying to determine whether there will be a transaction. Here is a recent situation that will help demonstrate the qualifying process involving a listing that I have for a family estate.

It started with a sign call. That innocuous little sign is actually an important advertising tool and the first step in qualifying a potential buyer for a real estate listing. I know, for example, that the fact that the house is on a busy street, in the flight pattern for an international airport, or is painted lime green is not a problem for her. So, back to my story, the prospective customer called my office on her way to work at 6:30 in the morning to inquire about specifics of the home. On my qualifying checklist, I now know that she is employed and, anybody who calls at 6:30 in the morning is serious about buying a house. I was able to determine her motivation via voice mail. I usually do not begin my workday at 6:30 am. Therefore, when I return her call, the buyer then learns the price, size, lay-out, number of rooms, and recent updates to the home. I likewise learn that my description of the home sounds appealing to the buyer, that she is married, has school-age children, her timing for the purchase, and the time that she leaves work so that an appointment to show the home can be scheduled. I do all of this in a conversational, non-threatening, comfortable, consultative (it is all about the customer) style. Now, I have a new best friend and an appointment for 4:30 the same afternoon. In the meantime, I have calculated the monthly payment for this home, based on rates available for folks with stellar credit.

It is important for the buyer to realize, if she is not already aware, the monthly payment. I can tell from body language—long pause on the phone or a gasp in shock—whether this prospective buyer is aware of exactly what she is getting into financially. So far, so good…she did not faint! Likewise, I learn that she has a condominium to sell and I offer to provide a market analysis for the condominium and bring the notes to our appointment in the afternoon. Also, I refer her to a mortgage banker for pre-approval. As it turned out, she had a previous financial relationship with my mortgage banker and was comfortable with my suggestion. Next, we meet to see the house at 4:30 and she wants to buy the house Right Now!!! I have learned during the course of our qualifying conversation that she is the decision-maker for this transaction. Though married, her husband has left the choice of a home strictly up to her; however, they must use both incomes to qualify for the purchase. Ok, that one item in our conversation tells me, based on experience, that a potential issue could arise in the mortgage qualifying process and I need further clarification from the mortgage banker before I am confident that the potential transaction is truly solid.

Both buyer and seller will use real estate attorneys for contract review as a stop-gap precaution early in the transaction; therefore, I must make sure that all details related to the transaction are in order before the attorney review begins. You already know how important qualifying each phase of the transaction can be to all the parties: the buyer and seller and the terms of the contract itself—then everybody is happy and the transaction closes. Wow! Are you ready for a real estate transaction?

So, let's summarize thus far. Qualify by establishing rapport. Qualify by determining intent of the buyer (i.e., wants a specific school district, four bedroom house, no pool, fenced yard, space for home office, etc). Qualify for decision-making capability. Qualify for financial stability. Qualify by continually offering services without an in-your-face style. Qualify by communicating and closing. The qualifying process is constant and takes place throughout the course of the transaction. I'm always looking for a way I can help with the next step or anticipate and prevent a potential crisis in the course of a transaction. Now, let me change the story a little since not everyone falls in love with the first house they see.

The first part is true: My client called, set an appointment, then hates the house, but likes me and wants my real estate services for the sale of her condominium and the purchase of a home. These two transactions will result in a simultaneous closing (the domino effect for transactions). From my side of the table, I have established rapport while demonstrating professionalism and market knowledge. I know, based on conversations with the buyer and communication with my mortgage banker that the buyer can qualify for a specific price range. The buyer needs a four bedroom home for her family and wants a five bedroom, but qualifies for a three bedroom home. Qualifying the wants and needs of the customer is part of the process as well because I'm working as a consultant for the buyer in the purchase of their next home. Additionally, I have another level of qualifying—the buyer for my condominium seller. Once the condominium sells, she becomes my buyer.

You get the picture. I need to know that the prospective buyer for my condominium listing—represented by another agent—is ready-willing-and able to purchase the listing so that my domino transaction does not crash. It can get a little complicated, so one must pay attention to the details. To me, a pre-qualification letter from a lender is a waste of paper. Ideally, I want "approved/subject to appraisal" language in the lender's letter in order to provide some level of confidence for my seller/buyer that their transactions will close on time and without last minute hysteria. I know, based on experience and market knowledge, that my contract price on the condominium will appraise, inspections will be satisfactory, and our side of the transaction will run smoothly. However, I need to know—so I can extend the same level of confidence to my seller—that their buyer is well qualified and will not have any mortgage underwriting issues, insurance issues, or other various and sundry last minute problems. As you can see, QUALIFYING is crucial. Constantly qualifying the transaction is crucial, but it's my job! Now, I've added another level to qualifying—the transaction. Is it viable and will it close on time? What else do I need to do in order to make sure that everyone else does their job in order to bring this transaction to fruition? I'm getting a little nervous just telling you about it.

However, in a worst-case scenario, the buyer loves the house and cannot qualify financially at this time. That is part of my consultative qualifying, as well. I always tell people—and it may sound corny—"if this house is meant to be for you, I will do everything in my power to make it happen for you." If not, when the timing is right, the finances are right, and the property is right, I will be there to help with every step of that transaction, too. It is my goal to make customers/clients feel comfortable with every step of the buying or selling process.

Ok, I've qualified the buyer, the seller, the seller's buyer. Based on previous experience through multiple transactions and with the various professionals associated with my transactions, I have pre-qualified each for their knowledge and abilities, these are the mortgage bankers, title companies, real estate attorneys and other agents associated with the various transactions in my day. Based on this qualifying data, I am confident that, unless something unforeseen occurs, my transactions will close and the buyer will be happy and so will the seller. My business has been founded on happy customers referring friends and family, and my initial consultative qualifying approach is the key to building long-standing relationships. Remember the Golden Rule—the true Golden Rule—treat people the way I want to be treated myself. This concept is important in Qualifying, too.

For me, each transaction is an exciting opportunity to help families become established in their next—and possibly—future homes. Qualifying helps with the next transaction, too, which is to my advantage for a long-standing real estate career. I am now very fortunate to be able to help the next generation of buyers and sellers. It is fun for me to help a single person, to attend their wedding, then their baby showers, sell their home and find a larger home as the family grows. Now, I'm helping their kids with their real estate needs (no, I'm not THAT old). And, it all starts with qualifying on a consultative level. My customers, clients and their extended family are comfortable in consulting me for real estate service for their residential needs and commercial real estate needs, too. That's the snowball effect of my business—it just keeps rolling along. In addition, my real estate family of customers Qualify their referrals, which helps me with Time Management.

Time Management is important in Qualifying, as well. I feel that it is important for each customer, client, and their extended family members to feel as though they are the most important person in my world. If they need a house or office space today or two years from now determines the level of immediate service or follow up time I will allow. Depending on the type of real estate product needed and the timing required for that particular transaction, qualifying the need through communication and market knowledge will help me provide the level of service that my people are used to receiving in each of their real estate transactions with me.

Remember, if you are the consumer in a real estate transaction, qualifying is important, too. You will qualify the property (sign call, advertisement, internet research, etc.), the real estate practitioner, the mortgage banker, the home inspector, and the area schools. It's a very big job. Obviously, establishing a comfortable relationship with a real estate professional will make other steps in the buying or selling process easier and less stressful for you.

Finally, I have to say, qualifying through a consultative approach has helped me establish long-standing relationships with my customers and clients. Actually, it is hard for me to call them customers when they become part of my family. With effective qualifying, I have been fortunate enough to build my real estate practice/family over the years. The good news in real estate, for me, retirement is not an option. I will have the good fortune to continue my practice for years to come by providing customer service through the continued use of my consultative qualifying style.

CONTACT INFORMATION:

Doris H. Houck, Realtor®
Licensed Real Estate Broker
P.R.I.S.M. Partners, Inc.
Preferred Real Estate Investments Sales and Marketing

CHAPTER 05

Negotiating with Owners

by DUSTY KEEFE

DUSTY KEEFE STARTED his business CAREER at the age of 18 in the field of direct sales. He opened his own branch office at 19 and was one of the most successful sales reps in the company. He trained and managed over 100 people working for him in his office and led it to be one of the top producing branch sales offices in the nation.

Keefe discovered real estate investing at the age of 21 and began a full time career with it shortly after leaving school. Since then, Keefe has studied and practiced all aspects of real estate investing, including advanced negotiating, lease options, subject-to's, owner financed deals, short sales, strategic marketing, foreclosures, property management, land trusts, personal property trusts, living trusts, using IRA money in real estate investing (tax free), and has a specialization in deal creation.

He credits much of his success to his family's support over the years, to his relentless pursuit of learning and to his mentors in business who guided him along the way.

Today Dusty Keefe is 25 years old and resides in the beautiful Charleston, SC area. He is a certified Master Practitioner of Neuro-Linguistic Programming and a full time real estate coach, consultant, and investor who spends his time working with students and on real estate related deals.

Negotiating with Owners

I'll never forget the best advice I ever received about creating wealth in real estate investing. When I first started, my mentor had been a full-time investor and teacher for over 25 years and was a millionaire many times over. He pulled me aside one day and said, "Becoming a millionaire in real estate investing is about only one thing...."

It's not a question of whether you will become a millionaire doing this. The only question is how many times you can repeat it during your investing career. The only fuel you will need to light this fire is a little bit of knowledge and time working on your side. It's not about buying a nice house in a nice area. It's not about curb appeal and it's not about finding the perfect rehab. It's not learning to find houses that are far under value or even learning how to deal with tenants.

It is a little bit of all of that, but the true secret to creating wealth in real estate investing is so simple that it has literally been around for millions of years. It is one word: **survival**. It is a mathematical certainty that you will be a multimillionaire if you read the concepts in this book and apply them over the next ten, twenty, and thirty years. Those who learn how to survive in this field over the years will be the ones who find themselves very wealthy at the end of the day..

This chapter teaches you how to survive with your real estate assets until retirement by using various negotiation strategies such as low-to-no-money down transactions, creative financing, and even having the seller pay you to by their house. Time can be your friend or your enemy in investing. We will discuss the techniques you need to put yourself into a position of being able to survive for many years with properties and to take advantage of time in order to achieve the lifestyle that you and your family have always dreamed of.

I have been fortunate enough to have had a lot of success at an early age by using the exact techniques this book discusses. My two best friends and I started reading about real estate investing during the summer before our last year in college. We bought our first investment property that fall while we were still in school, using pretty conventional methods. We sold that property a few months later and ended up collectively making about $70,000 on our first deal while we were still in school.

We were beginning to understand the power of real estate and what it was capable of bringing into our lives. We all decided to go to a Louis Brown seminar over that Christmas break in order to get a bigger picture of what was going on in the industry and to hone our skills as investors. By lunchtime on the first day of the seminar, we realized that going back to school for our last semester was completely out of the question. We were now full-time real estate investors. We waited until after Christmas had passed to break the exciting news to our parents about our new plans. Needless to say, they weren't as excited as we were about our newfound entrepreneurial spirit and ideas of real estate riches. They would soon be glad we didn't listen to them.

We soaked up all of the information we could from seminars, books, audio programs, and other investors. We got out there and practiced in the field every day until we started closing a few deals a month. We assigned certain roles in the business to the three of us and we became masterful at our specific assigned tasks. I had previous sales experience and had taught hundreds of people about sales and negotiating with the job I had in college, so I was assigned to be our negotiator. I have been negotiating full time ever since, and the rest, as they say, is history.

THE POWER OF SURVIVAL

There is absolutely no doubt in my mind that real estate is the best investment vehicle ever in the history of the world. How many real estate investors do you know who have been doing this job for twenty years who aren't incredibly rich? I can't even think of one. I know a handful of old-timers who either bought a few houses or some land in an amazing area that is now worth a small fortune. These guys had no idea what they were really doing. They most likely thought they needed to diversify and just wanted some basic rental income, had some farm land that their families worked, or just wanted to supplement their salaries from their full-time jobs. They stumbled into a very comfortable retirement for themselves...and sometimes for their kids, too.

All of us probably know of some real estate old-timers who own 25 or so houses that they have accumulated over the past thirty years— all free and clear! He or she probably bought these houses for close to full price using conventional methods but figured out how to survive over the years until these assets paid off and provided some real flexibility for their lifestyles. For example, if somebody owns 25 houses that are paid off and is receiving $1,000 per month in rent from these houses, then they have a cash flow of $25,000 per month in income (not including taxes and insurance payments). That is serious passive income—true wealth. Whether they choose to work or not, this money still pours in every month.

I have had contact with an investor in Arizona who owns 300 single family houses, almost all of which are paid for...imagine that! These investors were everyday people who operated in a time before real estate courses, gurus, and real instructions. And yet they still somehow figured out how to survive until their portfolios were worth an unimaginable fortune. There is even more opportunity today and it is all around us.

SETTING YOURSELF UP FOR SUCCESS

Make sure you are meeting with the right kind of people. Never get mad at yourself for not getting a signed contract when you're meeting with an un-motivated seller. If you're going to beat yourself up about something, then get mad that you were there in the first place. Don't waste time on people who don't need your service. You should only drive to a house to meet with a seller if you are positive they are motivated to do business with you and need to have the deal completed yesterday. There are too many people who would beg to do business with you no matter what market you are in. There is nothing worse than leaving your home or office, fighting traffic, driving all the way to somebody's house, going through your whole proposal, and then realizing that you were DOA (dead on arrival) from the first moment you arrived. In this case, you never had a chance and it would be the investor's fault for not pre-qualifying enough before you chose to meet with these people. Half of negotiating is getting in front of the right people in the first place. Dealing only with highly motivated sellers will make you look like a negotiating genius.

It is vital that you ensure that all the decision makers are present every time you go to a house. This ensures that you can leave with a deal in your hand. A good place to start is asking the seller to please tell you all the names of the people who are on the title and whether or not there is anybody else who will be involved in the decision-making process of selling this property. If so, those people should probably be present when you meet with everyone about how to move forward. If their uncle is a realtor and he's not on the title but they pass all real estate decisions through him for approval, then get him there, too. I can't think of how many times I have arrived at a house all fired up to make a deal, sat down with everybody who was there, come to a resolution and then realized I didn't have all the necessary people to sign off or make a decision at that moment. There are few things in the world that are more frustrating than coming to a great deal with half of the people involved and then having to explain the same situation all over again later to the other half as why they should sell to you for the price and terms you thought you already negotiated. Be sure to have everybody there the first time you meet.

Negotiating great real estate deals is the single most important thing that we can do as investors. Many books say that you should meet with 100 sellers in person before buying one good deal. This idea is ridiculous. These authors should be invoiced for all the time they have caused to be wasted. Your time is now much too valuable to adhere to such a system. Your job is to slay dragons, to get out there in the field, and to get things done.

With the exception of marketing and negotiating, I would highly recommend eventually delegating all other tasks in real estate investing. You are not a handyman. Don't let a plunger touch your hands unless you desire to be paid like a plumber. Don't swing a hammer unless you want to be paid like a construction worker. Don't put your hands in the dirt unless you want to be paid like a gardener. There is absolutely nothing wrong with these professions; they just are not our path. Your time is most effectively spent negotiating with highly motivated sellers who will beg to do business with you.

YOUR MINDSET

When you are attending a meeting with a motivated seller it's very important to get into the right mindset for a deal to be created. These people deserve your best, so clear your mind of everything but their business. Stay completely focused on helping to resolve their real estate issues.

Maybe listening to one of your favorite songs on the way to the house gets you in a great mood. Maybe it's thinking of another time that you created a great deal and you were on fire when you were leaving that appointment thinking of your accomplishment. If you are still working on your first deal, then think about leaving an appointment and imagine the perfect outcome of that appointment, how nice the sellers were to you, how helpful you were to them, and how all this unfolded so effortlessly.

I do this every time... for every appointment... without exception. This is my pre-game ritual and now it can be yours. This is guaranteed to release any pre-negotiation stress that may arise and allows you to focus completely on the task at hand. The negotiation is already over in my mind before it even begins. The perfect outcome has already come to fruition.

Your client will always pick up what you are projecting. You must know before ever setting foot into that house that you are the best possible thing that could happen to these people and that they are lucky that you have come to meet with them

We have the opportunity and privilege to make some real positive changes in families' lives and are trusted to do so in many cases. Always do what you say you will and you won't have any trouble in this game. Know that you are the best and most efficient problem solver in your town and the seller will know it also.

MEETING WITH THE SELLER

We have put together a simple formula for negotiating great deals that adheres to the K.I.S.S (Keep it simple stupid) method. We call these three easy-to-remember steps "The Rapid Selling Technique."

Step One: Build massive Rapport.
Step Two: Build overwhelming value in what you're offering.
Step Three: Ask for what you want.

STEP ONE: BUILD MASSIVE RAPPORT

The very first step in successful negotiating is creating rapport with the seller. This begins with your very first contact with that person, whatever form you use. My appointments are pre-screened and set up by my office so I always go out of my way to call the person when I'm on the way over and introduce myself and ask specific directions, even if I know where I'm going. This gives me my first shot at building rapport with this person and creates the perception that we're on the same team working together to accomplish something. Then I arrive at the house and meet them at the door with a big smile and a handshake. I always ask for a glass of water or a cup of coffee when I arrive, just something that has become part of my rapport-building pattern. I believe it helps the seller to become more comfortable and start to accept you as part of the house and lets them know you're planning on sticking around for awhile or until you've come to a resolution for their situation. Perhaps more importantly, it also sets the stage that when you ask for something they respond by being open to the idea of giving it to you. It's the first "yes" from them in a series of many more to follow.

I never mention real estate or buying houses to them until they do. I use this time to build massive rapport and gather information about who I'm working with by getting to know them on a personal level. Don't rush this building rapport step because it is so important. Building "initial rapport" is the foundation for the rest of the negotiation. If they don't like you, they simply won't do business with you—no matter what their situation is.

You can also build in something I call "deep rapport" on an unconscious level by doing a series of things. This technique will allow you to build trust rapidly with whoever you are working with very quickly and efficiently. (This topic is covered more thoroughly in a free Audio CD available at www. FreeNegotiatingCD.com).

STEP TWO: BUILD OVERWHELMING VALUE IN WHAT YOU'RE OFFERING.

Okay, they love you...now what? It is time to move on to building value in what you're there to do. When the seller finally brings up the fact that you're there to see the house, I advise walking around with them and letting them show you what really needs attention. Usually I just compliment the good things that I see and maybe say, "Yeah, every house could probably use a little work and money poured into it…this one's no different. Overall I think it's a fine house that could have potential." Mainly, I want the sellers to know that I have seen the whole house so in their minds they will have made the connection that there is a good reason behind the number I say when I am ready to make an offer.

I'm completely focused on the seller's needs and the appointment when I'm there. The physical house is not that important to me, but I do care a lot about the underlying deal. The numbers are what is most important at this time.

I have learned that the best way to kill their suspicion about your intentions is to be completely honest with sellers. I say, "John and Jane, I want to be real straightforward with you and I hope you'll do the same for me. The company I work with has to see some kind of way they can make a profit by buying this house in order for this to work. Is that going to be any kind of a problem for you? They typically have to be able to buy a property at around 65-70% of value to make the numbers work in a way that will make sense for them. Obviously they'd have to figure out someway to be able to make a profit doing this or we wouldn't be able to stay in business very long. Does that make sense? And to be honest, John and Jane, at this point I'm not even sure this would qualify as something they'd be interested in. But we'll give it our best shot today to put something together to present to them while we're all here together right now."

This is a powerful phrase. We have now established that we are in the reluctant role, and the least motivated person in any negotiation usually ends up on top. The idea is that it really doesn't matter to us or our company whether we buy the property or not. We are going to have to "qualify" the house to see if it is even something in which "they"(the company) might be interested. At the same time, we are actually planting the seeds that if we are interested, then the house will be put under contract today.

I actually take out the purchase contract and as we talk and I find out what's important to them. I'll say, "Let me make a note of that" and I'll write it right on the contract. By the end of the meeting, the contract is already filled out. I go on to say, "Their job in the office is to make sure that buying this property makes good business sense and that it will work for them. My entire job is making sure that it works for you. So I'm interested in finding out your exact goals and time frames. I'm only interested in working together if this can be a win-win situation. One where the company can do okay and you are going to be a raving fan and tell all your friends about how great it was to work with us after we have finished. Does that sound fair?"

So now you are both on the same side of the table presenting the possibility of a deal to "them," the people in the office who will have the final say-so. This is a very powerful tactic called the *higher authority negotiation technique*. If the sellers try to press you in any way, then you can always remind them that it's not up to you, it's up to the boss—but you'll be happy to ask.

Handle any objections that may arise before they come up. To accomplish this I will often say, "There are a couple outcomes from a meeting like this, if I figure out that we are not a good fit to do business together do you mind if I just tell you? At the same time if you figure out this isn't something you're interested in will you just go ahead and tell me? Often people say things like 'let me think it over' or 'I'll call you next week' or 'I have to run it by my brother.' If you're not interested, can we just call it what it is, which is a *No* and move on with no hard feelings? Great. Now let's see what we can do here." In almost all cases this gets rid of any stalling objections later in the appointment because they don't want to use an excuse that you've already covered with them as being not an acceptable outcome to the meeting.

Now our goal is to find out what they perceive as the best way to move forward. *What do they believe has to happen in their near future? How much money, if any, are they expecting out of this transaction? What are they doing with the money? Do they need it to get into an apartment, or for a storage place for their things, or to pay off credit card bills?* This is valuable information to know for several reasons. One is that you can possibly show them a way they don't need as much money as they thought. Second, they are sharing with you what is going on inside their minds so you can show them how you could make this happen and bring some kind of resolution to their situation.

Ask, "If getting rid of this property could work out perfectly for you, how would that look to you?" Find out what their true motivators are: *Is it* time? Do they need to close in 5 days? Are they getting foreclosed on in a week? Is it money? Do they need $7k by next Friday? Are they behind on their kids' tuition? Is it dealing with deadbeat tenants? Find out what their true motivations are for selling because that is how to build overwhelming value in what you have to offer. You can close in 3 days if need be. You can pay them a few grand by the end of the week. You can buy the house as-is so they don't have to make the repairs. You aim to please and you are a professional problem solver. You have demonstrated massive value in what you have to offer.

STEP THREE: ASK FOR WHAT YOU WANT

We have to ask ourselves what we want, or what would be valuable to me as an investor? Some things that come to mind are great prices; lots of equity; easy, flexible buying terms. I have never, not even once to date, used my credit or my own money to buy a house. Not ever. I've also never paid interest on any seller-held or owner-financed notes. That is quite a statement after buying hundreds of houses, but my point is that anybody can create millions out of "nothing" if you know what to ask for.

Most real estate negotiating material will tell you that you are always negotiating two things: price and terms. I've always chosen to think of this a little differently. I think about the two factors that we are negotiating with motivated sellers as *equity* and *terms* rather than as *price* and *terms* Obviously the overall price that we are paying is important to us, but is not usually a real sticking point for the seller. If you are dealing with a highly motivated seller, they usually are not demanding a certain sales price. The seller is more concerned with how much equity, if any, they are obtaining and when they will be receiving it. . And if they are concerned about actual sales price then I will usually reframe the conversation to one about how much actual money that means to them at closing. I rarely fill in the sales price until the end of the meeting. (My forms have one blank for the seller's equity and a separate line for the sales price.)

We already know what their house is worth and we know their mortgage balance before we ever meet with them, so we already have a clear understanding of how much equity could be involved. The equity is there, it is just a matter of how much we are going to pay them for it. We find out if getting out from under this debt would make them happy. They might say yes, or they might say they need to get out from under the debt and net $5k. Your goal is to come to the closing table with least amount of money possible. You might ask, "How much of the $5k would you need at closing and how much could you take in a promissory note?" This could result in a no money down transaction where we take over their loan payments and give them a note for their equity due.

Another form of a no money down deal that we have used with great success is not only taking over someone's payments, but asking them to make 2-3 (or however many) of the next payments for you to make the deal work. This greatly helps your cash flow because not only do you not have an underlying payment on the property for these months, you could also be collecting rent from a tenant and enjoying 100% cash flow for the months you have negotiated. This is getting paid to buy a house, and happens often if you will ask for it.

My favorite is when the seller writes one big check just to get rid of a problem property. We closed on a house a couple of months ago where the numbers just weren't going to work unless the seller brought a large check to closing to make up the difference. The seller was so tired of the property that she brought a certified check from her personal bank account to closing for a little over $26k just to rid herself of this problem property. She even gave us hugs at the closing table for taking it over! We were actually paid over $26k up front to buy that house! Amazing! Yet it happens all the time when you ask for (and expect) what you want from the deal.

Every once and awhile you will find a seller who thinks they are really ready to do something with their house and then you get there and they are still hung up on wanting close to retail price. This is rare if you pre-qualify properly, but does happen from time to time. I have a way to deal with these situations as well. I simply ask them "Have you ever had the opportunity to price how much it actually costs to sell a home before?" Then I go through the traditional costs and time frames associated with selling a property with them on a worksheet for them to see. They might be asking 100K for their house, so I write that at the top of our sheet. Under that are all the expenses that we are going to point out based on a six month holding period, including realtor commission (6%), closing fees (3%), Holding costs (about 6 months of mortgage payments), property taxes for six months, etc. When you do the math it might add up to around 25k of expenses to hold it for an extra 6 months while trying to sell it for that higher price. When I know they understand this completely then I will ask, "If you were able to net the same thing next week instead of in six months...would that work for you?" This would be a standard case of buying a house for 75k when they were asking 100k (75% of value). This is a very conservative example that happens often and is a great way to create a nice equity spread that didn't exist before you made it happen through your negotiating skills.

Negotiating great terms is probably my favorite way to buy property. If done correctly, it allows you to buy a deal with little to no money, be able to hold through the few short years until the property is paid for completely, and bring money in for the rest of your life. We bought a house a few years ago for 36k that is worth 80k, but the real deal here is that we actually pay the seller only 6k per year for six years to buy the property at zero percent interest. That means we bought the house for no money down and pay it completely off in six years. I've used this strategy to buy middle to low end homes and pay them off very quickly, and I've used it to buy a million dollar beach home that I still own—all with no money down.

I am always asking for two things: a nice chunk of equity and the most forgiving and flexible terms imaginable. There is nothing that says you can't have both. You can be as creative as you want with the terms of how you purchase properties. Also, don't forget to ask for "the stuff" when buying a property. We have even had personal property thrown into the deal like pool tables, big screen TVs, boats, jet skis, furniture, and appliances. These can be sold, kept or even rented to the next tenant for additional sources of income!

Most importantly, always remember to make the other party feel like they "won" the negotiation. The true art of negotiating is taking every situation you're presented with and turning it in to a "win-win" transaction for everybody involved. When you learn how to effectively perform this in every negotiation then you will be blessed with everything in life you could ever desire.

GO GET STARTED

It is my hope that you were able to draw some helpful information about negotiating that will start to change your financial picture and get you closer to where you want to be.

One of my missions when I work with people is to make a positive impact on their lives. I look forward to hearing about your progress and prosperity. God bless and happy investing!

CONTACT INFORMATION & ADDITIONAL RESOURCES:

Dusty Keefe, CRI, CTS, CDS
Professional life coach and Certified Practitioner of NLP

For more information about Dusty Keefe's ongoing programs and services or to schedule a student interview for his coaching program his office may be contacted at (843) 849-8991.
Fax: (843) 849-7087

To obtain a copy of his free CD, *7 Things You Must Know Yesterday about Negotiating Great Deals*, please visit **www.FreeNegotiatingCD.com**

Making Offers/ Strategies for Making Offers

by BRYAN CRABTREE

Bryan Crabtree was born on February 18, 1977 in Nashville, Tennessee. After graduating with honors from Springfield High School, Crabtree went on to attend Austin Peay State University under the President's Emerging Leaders Program and later The University of Memphis. Crabtree, worked in programming and management for Citadel Communications and SFX broadcasting, now Clear Channel – The Nation's largest broadcaster.

Having multiple levels of business, marketing and management experience, Crabtree began a real estate career in 1999 for Coldwell Banker and later founded Dean-Kelby Realty LLC which began a franchise relationship with Weichert, Realtors in early 2003.

Weichert, Realtors is America's Largest Independent Real Estate Company, and "was exactly what this market [and my business] needed to improve the overall level of professionalism," says Crabtree. "Weichert is a 30 year heritage company that's been doing business right with the customer and the highest level of integrity – That's what excites me most about real estate!" Crabtree's excitement for real estate has awarded him the Realtor Executive Roundtable award more than once; This award is the highest accolade of service, production volume, education and integrity a Tri-County Realtor can receive.

Crabtree's experience stems from marketing and market research which helps provide marketing plans for the smallest home to the largest development.

His business and management background combined with his financial expertise and sales savvy, provides his personal clients and those of the company with
service and results that are second to none. As an owner of a local Corporation
and LLC, combined with his own business ventures and investment strategies,
client's find "new-age" and innovative ways to market, buy and sell real estate.

Making Offers / Strategies for Making Offers

In our radio series, we frequently discuss the art of making offers. I believe that you make money in real estate when you buy. When you "buy right" you set the course for the profit you desire to realize when you sell. Selling a property costs you money: commissions, closing costs, capital gains, income tax. We frequently believe selling is when money is lost. In fact, money is lost at the sale due to the costs associated. Therefore, to effectively negotiate a contract for purchase, a buyer must employ skill, strategy and technique.

Recently, one of my associates shared a story with me that highlights the critical functions of a skilled negotiator. I was very proud that we had been able to save a client (earn a client) so much extra money. A contract for purchase on a property was ratified at $700,000. According to the appraisal, the value was only $500,000. The buyer's agent issued a letter stating that the buyer would split the difference (from appraised to contract price) with the seller, pay $600,000, and continue with the purchase of the property. The buyer's agent told us that the "buyer really wants the property." This is our first example of a big mistake in negotiating. Knowing our seller's needs, our agent spoke with the seller and explained that he thought the buyer would pay more (even in light of the fact that the contract was contingent on an appraisal). He suggested $650,000, presented the counter-offer to the buyer and it was accepted. The buyer ended up paying even more, because the seller didn't want to pay any of his closing costs. He wanted to net $650,000. Knowing that the buyer wanted all the funds possible for his move to Florida our firm called the dual-agent representing the buyer (our seller) and the seller of the new property in Florida and explained the trouble in the deal. The contract in Florida was contingent upon the sale of our client's current home and the agent there was concerned about the closing. In that market, there was a heavy supply of homes and the dual-agent, interested in closing the deal and not losing the sale, convinced the seller to reduce the price of that home another $15,000.

The above example represents a lot of skilled-negotiation by one party and a tremendous lack by the others. Our seller lost money on the sale: $50,000 from the original contract price (re: market but not appraisal value). In fairness, the buyer of his property lost $150,000. In other words, he paid $150,000 more than the property was currently valued. Our seller also earned an additional $15,000 on the purchase of his new home in Florida. Net loss? $35,000. He made up the difference on the buying side (by buying right) This concepts sounds odd doesn't it? I forgot to mention that he paid $80,000 for the property that was sold for $650,000. Therefore, the real money made was the true appreciation since the purchase. He couldn't control the pricing factors on the sale of his home (the market sets the price). But, he was the market on the purchase of his home in Florida, and he set the price.

The buyer, who paid $150,000 more than appraisal, actually lost money on the purchase. Emotions and poor negotiations resulted in a sale for a price far more than the property's value.

There are several lessons that can be learned from this scenario:

1. Stop talking! State your position and add nothing more. We all have a tendency to spray too much information.

2. Do not get emotionally attached to a property.

3. Identify a skilled negotiator. If you are negotiating with someone that "seems" to be doing a good job for themselves or their client, then there is a good chance that there is more "wiggle-room" than they are stating.

4. Always be willing to walk from a deal to see if the last offer is the best offer.

5. If you are found in a situation where things aren't coming together, be willing to make up the difference from all sides (re: negotiating on the seller-side and buyer-side of the subject properties in which you are involved).

6. Always put a layer between you and the decision. (Re: I must speak with my business partner, attorney, Realtor, before making a final decision). Adding a layer allows you to take a position of "I'll get back to you," instead of "I'm capable of making an immediate decision." Trust me, you'll cave under the pressure of the latter.

7. The best deals (as a buyer) happen if you slow down. Once a contract is written, the buyer is in control as long as you are within the timelines identified in the contract.

When making offers, negotiating contract clauses and presenting, you should state your position, provide the facts and walk away. Do not continue talking. Answer questions very matter-of-fact and stop at that. I have a phrase I use in training classes: "Every time you open your mouth in a negotiation, you lose Five-Grand." Remember that phrase the next time you have the urge to talk with a seller about anything other than the specific terms in the contract.

Emotion. People buy homes to either move away from pain or toward pleasure. And, both cost you money unless you remove the emotional components from the decision. Before making an offer, set a price you are willing to pay, and do not accept terms or price that are more than $1 over where you've set "the bar." I've seen people buy a home just to get started in investments; the first one they see. The most successful investors and homebuyers will look at a hundred or more homes before ever buying one. Instead of viewing this tiring search as a waste of time, look at it as an education. If you've seen 100-200 homes in an area, chances are you've done more research than the average Realtor. I tell our new agents to start previewing homes until they are so busy showing them to clients, they can't preview any more. A professional real estate associate, investor or owner should always be looking at homes and only buying those that are "deals." How do you know a deal when you see it? You've seen so many that aren't, you'll have no doubt, and no emotion; after a while it's just "bricks and sticks." Buying right becomes an instinct.

Skilled Negotiations. If you're doing a deal with a seller or an agent (representing the seller), identify early whether they are skilled or unskilled. If they start telling you about the seller/buyer's personal situation, needs, wants, they are unskilled. If they focus on the value, market-conditions or supporting components to their price, they are skilled. Therefore, a person talking about their personal needs, situation or wants is probably telling the truth when they say this is "as low as I'll go." By contrast, when a seller (for instance) that seems quite skilled may leave a lot of room on the table when he/she says, "this is as low as I'll go." Be prepared to walk, they may just chase you down.

The first one to speak loses. If you've been made a counter-offer to an offer you've made a seller and the seller calls you to see if you have a response, you've won. Likewise, if you make an offer to the seller and you call he/she back to see what their response is, you lose. Remember? Every time you open your mouth it costs you "Five Grand." Do not get anxious; wait!

Be willing to walk from a deal if you don't get a response. You may lose it, or the seller may be chasing another deal that will end similar to yours. Don't worry, once they run the other buyer off, or the deal fails, they'll call you more desperate than before. "But, what if I lose the property?" If it was lost at terms higher than "your bar," you shouldn't be concerned. Look for the next one. Remember, you may have to engage in some part of this process 100 times to find the best deals in town.

Making up the difference from both sides. In our example, earlier in this chapter, we discussed how a skilled negotiator in my company made it up on both sides. He leveraged the facts of the sale to save our seller money on his next purchase. How? He knew all the facts. The other negotiators gave up too much information. Our agent did not. The result? $15,000 in additional savings to the buyer. In this case, the seller of the new property, must have opened his/her mouth three times too many. "Five-grand each!"

Other ways to "make up the difference" are in negotiations on personal property. Frequently, you can get washers, dryers, refrigerators, old cars, swing-sets and more simply by throwing it in the contract. These items also elicit the sellers' willingness to "open their mouth." Cha-ching! "Five Grand." They'll tell you why they need to take them; money, new home, situation, job situation, family situation. And, if not, they'll throw them in for free. For a seller, these things are a liability in the move. For a buyer, they're a cost-savings of thousands. The old car? Check with your accountant; it may be a tax deduction for you. Whether it's your home or an investment, personal property has an intrinsic value that can't be beaten.

Layers of negotiation. Have you ever noticed how hard it is to get something done at a government office? And, by the time you finally get the answer (which is usually what you don't want to hear), your defeated at this point, swallow it and agree to whatever it is, just to get it over. That's called layers of negotiation. Basically, they make it so difficult to deviate from their "norm" that you'll give up and accept it. Now, I'm not saying to enter that level of government bureaucracy into your own negotiation, but a little lesson from Uncle Sam couldn't hurt. If you get an offer you don't like and aren't currently willing to accept, you have two options:

1. Immediately counter with acceptable terms.

2. "This sounds possible, but I'll have to run it by my (attorney, wife, business partner, etc). I might add, "I'm pretty confident they will accept 'X,' and if you can do that, I'm sure we'll have a deal." This way you become a seeming advocate of the opposing party and your attorney, wife, business partner is the layer that saves you money. If they don't agree immediately, let them "sweat it out" while you employ one of the best negotiators in the real estate business: time.

Adding a layer of negotiation between you and the final decision is a must. I've found that it's much easier to have one of my agents represent me in my own seller transactions, because it's much easier to say "no" and let them deliver the message. This way, their reasoning can have little to no influence on my decision-making. Buyers can learn your needs/wants and play with them, if they are too close to you in the transaction.

Slow down. Have you ever heard of the 9-1-1 call about the real estate emergency? You probably haven't and you probably won't. There is no "ER" for real estate. Many of us want to get the deal done so quickly that we'll lose money in the process of rushing. Real estate is a game of patience. It takes patience to build long-term growth and wealth. And, it takes patience to complete the deal that produces instant equity at closing. It's the seller's haste as a buyer that created the situation that made him so motivated to sell. You may be asking, "what haste?" For instance, the seller's credit card debt (they couldn't wait to buy that big-screen), the car that doesn't work, but has two years worth of payments on it (they paid too much), the $50,000 kitchen renovation in a $120,000 house (they wanted the features of the mansion before they could afford it), and the swimming pool in the back yard (jacuzzi on top). And, you, the investor/buyer now have to move a dead car, redo the kitchen again (who picked those colors?) and fill in the pool. For all that work, maybe they'll throw in the big screen!

Do you see it? It's not enough to have the American Dream. Today, we get "the dream" and immediately start spending it. So, now they have to sell to pay off all this stuff, and you are the one person willing to bail them out. Taking advantage? Not really! The seller needs out because they were in a hurry to have everything and to own everything, but now they can't pay for it. As it relates to real estate, taking your time and going slow is always a winner. They won't see their own mistakes and immediate needs as much as you will.

Now that you have the contract, you have inspections, appraisals and more. And, many times while the seller was installing the pool and renovating the kitchen, they were missing the termites and the roof leaks. This is the second phase of negotiating. Unless you are buying the property as-is, you have to realize that this is a stage of the game that will either make you a lot of money or cost you your profit (or even worse: lose you money). I have a general rule of thumb on repairs:

> **The total high-cost of all repairs, doubled, is the concession I want. Even if you're doing the work yourself, you should price the market-cost of labor into your negotiations. Your time is worth money. If you're only going to deduct the cost of the repairs (that you will complete) from the price, then why not buy the property at market value, in good condition, down the street?**

Be willing to back out of a contract at this stage even more rapidly than in the initial stage. I "fell in love" with a condo about 5 years ago. I bought it, even though the price was higher than my "bar," the issues were too numerous and the feeling of its condition just wasn't right. $125,000 in repairs and

9 months in rent (having to move out) later, I finally got a problem-free unit. Well, not really. Because they stripped the entire outside of the building and left it exposed to the elements, the A/C unit died, the hot water heater quit working, as did the dishwasher and garbage disposal. Make that $130,000 later. In retrospect, I did make good money when it sold. But compared to similar property in the area, the opportunity costs of using so much money for the down-payment and repairs made it a mediocre deal in the end.

So, you "make your money when you buy." It might be best said that you make your money in negotiations with the seller. The more you negotiate, the more you win. Follow the steps outlined in this chapter when you negotiate and you'll make more on the purchase. And, keep in mind, that a large list of problems uncovered in your inspection is likely to result and big-discount.

Most people are ready to shed their problems at a discounted rate when they're uncovered. And, if they don't? They're likely to have to disclose these new problems in advance to a new buyer or spend the money up front to fix them before the new buyer gets involved. Either way, it's a difficult move for a seller to know they have latent structural defects and have your contract released. There's always a chance they'll come back to you when another buyer doesn't want to buy their problems.

Remember, when you're buying you must always stay in control (even in a Seller's market). If not, you'll pay too much or inherit a costly problem. As a seller, you'll lose money in order to "cash-in" and realize the gain. And, that's okay. Real Estate is a business transaction, and if you focus on the business aspect (the dollars and cents), while making informed/intelligent decisions, you'll make more money than you ever thought possible.

PART II

Tax sales can be a very profitable venture. In November 2004, I visited the Charleston County Tax Sale in South Carolina. At the time, our real estate market was "red-hot" so there were over 300 people at this sale. After a morning of bidding, and being outbid, I was beginning to think "giving up" might be my best option. Shortly, after lunch, the room was half-full and the sale continued. A property in a popular area of Charleston called James Island came up for sale. I bought it for $32,000. It had a current-value of about $155,000.

Recently, on the radio show, I conducted a tax sale advisement series. Donald, a listener, asked the follow question:

> **"After your show... I talked to someone about tax sales that had an interesting question. What about any unpaid mortgages, leans etc. I heard of a tax sale where the EPA charged the new owner millions for a clean up. Thanks, Donald"**

You have to quiet the title with an attorney, which involves a "legal" process. But in a correctly structured tax sale purchase, a mortgage disappears. I would suggest the investment into John Beck's Tax Sale Program. http://www.johnbeck.net. It's about $50.

Also, be aware, that the 12% interest is calculated based on:

12% of the amount owed so long as the interest does not exceed the back taxes and penalties (for SC).

Re: $2500 in taxes due—you buy property for $35,000 with a value of $125,000. Twelve per cent of $35,000 is $4200. You would only earn $2500 if they bought the property back in the 11th month.

Taxes in SC are paid: 3% if redeemed in the first 3 months, 6% 3-6, 9% 6-9 and the 12% in the 9-12 month range.

Let me explain my 2004 Charleston Real Estate tax sale experience. I visited the courthouse in Charleston County along with about 350 other people. After lunch, the room was half full and I bought a condo on James Island and a lot in North Charleston, SC for a total of $41,000. The lot was bought back by the original owner (during the redemption period) and we made $948 interest that year (or about 9.5%). See above for why 9.5% not 12%.

The condo wasn't bought back. So, we proceeded to the attorney to quiet the title. Apparently, the original owner had decided to put it up for sale sometime after I bought it. In doing so, his potential agent told him he didn't own it any longer. He called wanting me to sell it back for what I paid for it. Obviously, I said no. However, with a value of $210,000, and no mortgage, I knew he was willing to fight the battle. So, my choice was "spend two years to win and $30,000 more in legal fees (with a slight potential of actually losing the case and the fees), or sell it back to him for (I thought it was fair), double what I paid plus interest. He took the latter option after I offered, and I walked out with an 18 month profit on 32,000 invested with $68,500 (including interest). I put that down on an under priced piece of property, which I now have rented. No hassles, no lawsuits. In this case, negotiation was based on legal facts and advisement. The old saying goes: "Pigs get fed and Hogs get slaughtered," I chose to be a pig on this one.

In real estate investing, it's better to always take the side of the "pig," because the "hog" just never seems to be profitable. The immediate power of money in real estate is important verses the uncertainty of legal proceedings.

My thinking is that the tax sale is for someone with lots of cash and no idea what to do with it. It's fun, it takes a long time but the payout is great. I heard once you could double your cash every two-three years in tax sales. I believe it. But, I believe in the cash leverage side of smart real estate buying. I'm in more control that way. But, the tax sale may be just right for you. Also, read the "Rich Dad Poor Dad" Series by Robert Kiyosaki; he made millions in tax sales.

PART III.

I found that there are a lot of ways to make money and create wealth in real estate. Some of them include:

1. Foreclosure Acquisitions

2. Real Estate Brokerage Sales

3. Tax-Sale Properties

4. Flipping / Speculative Purchasing

5. Commercials Ownership

6. Residential Landlord

7. Long-term Holds

8. Lease purchases

9. Development

10. Land

11. Land Redevelopment

12. Purchase and Renovate

And, there are many more.

The biggest negotiation that occurs in most anyone's real estate endeavors is with themselves. I've been guilty of trying to do all twelve of the above, at once. It's stressful, unfocused and lacks complete productivity. The twelve scenarios, above, could be listed as doctor, lawyer, accountant, etc. Those careers all involve people, right? The "scenarios" involve real estate. You may focus on more than one in your career, but it's reasonable to say that you can only do one or two areas of real estate really well.

For instance, if you are going to be the "Foreclosure Acquisition King," then there's a lot of work and focus needed. First, you have to advertise. There's nothing better than the "We Buy Houses" signs, assuming your local ordinances allow them. I would get about 12 calls per month off those signs (and it could take as much as 2-3 months for one of those calls to become something viable). Then, there's plain "cold-calling." Most county websites have a *lis pendens* list (litigation pending) as it relates to real property. Using the county site and an online search (re: www.whitepages.com), I could usually find the owner. It may take 100 calls, contacts and/or inquiries to produce just one viable lead that leads to an equitable purchase. And, you need to get laser-sharp at recognizing the costs, time and skills associated with those 100 calls. As you can see, 100 calls per week (20 per day) could net you a very healthy equity position if 100 calls equals one equitable deal. But, if you're focus is torn between land, development, lease purchases, foreclosures and a host of other activities, you will lack focus and likely a lack of results will follow.

In this chapter, we've talked about negotiation. If you make/receive 100 calls, and one of them (statistically) is viable, negotiation skills are key in closing the deal. Generally, the foreclosure calls I've made or received were people who:

1. Didn't pay their mortgage

2. Didn't do anything about it until the court date was set (they were in denial)

3. Doesn't have anywhere to live

4. Doesn't understand the process for which they are embarking (with foreclosure)

5. Can't make a decision

6. Has very little time

7. Has some equity (usually in property appreciation)

8. And, doesn't care about, well, anything

Now the above eight may be a bit sensationalized, but those are the ones I bought. Knowing that someone is about to be homeless, has no money, can't make a decision, doesn't understand and is about to lose their most valuable asset, there is really not much negotiation needed here. They need me/you assuming we have money and can close fast.

In being ethically and morally correct, if I can put a little money in their pocket, help them with a place to live (or give them 60 days free rent after I close), pick up the property at 70-80% of market value and help them stop a foreclosure, we've both encountered a true "win-win." In order to have this happen, I must educate them on the process of foreclosure, what I do and how this can effect them. By doing this, I build trust and show them that I'm not just here to make money, I'm here to help where I can.

You can also agree to reinstate the loan (by paying the delinquent amounts to the bank), stop the foreclosure and buy time for one of three options:

1. Buy the property with cash raised from outside investors

2. Buy the property with a conventional mortgage at a competitive rate

3. Develop a trust, assuming payments of their mortgage and releasing them from the obligation

The latter option can be a very nice source of easy-money for acquiring real estate. However, it's important to realize, it's also complicated and has very strict legal requirements that are different in each state. So, consult an attorney and do some reading. Sites like www.thecreativeinvestor.com, can offer some useful tips.

For more useful advice on real estate investing, you can listen to segments of our weekly WTMA radio show and read my blogsite at www.realestateshowblog.com. There's usually 3-4 new investment topics per week posted.

CONTACT INFORMATION:

Call Bryan with all of your real estate needs at (843) 607-7355 or email: **bryan@housedog.com**

FINANCING

by ADRIAN MIKELIUNAS

Adrian is an internationally acclaimed speaker, loan officer, and trainer.

Having a solid education both in Spanish and French from Le Lycée Français of Montevideo, Uruguay, and after careful analysis of the computer field, Adrian decided to focus both on computers and their business applications when he arrived in New York in 1979. Towards that endeavor, first he obtained a Computer Diploma from the Grumman Data System Institute in Long Island, NY. Then he received his BS in Business Administration from Bloomfield College while working at the University of Medicine and Dentistry in Newark, NJ. Then he received a BS in Computer Science from Kennedy Western University, where he is currently pursuing his MBA.

Adrian has been an IT instructor for the past ten years for the George Washington University, the Learning Tree International and Megamind. For the past fifteen years he has been involved with the International Monetary Fund and The World Bank Group as an independent computer consultant. As a technical expert, he has been in several video conferences and appearances including "CNN en Español" and "Conversemos esta Noche", from Worldnet TV Spanish (Voice of America.)

Adrian has turned his attention closer to home, to personal and real estate financing for the past few years. He is currently involved with local Real Estate investors groups. His customers range from international chefs, business owners, investors and first time home buyers. The most critical component of the loan is customer education, making sure the customer understands all the options available and help him or her make the right decision.

As a loan officer with Pinnacle Financial, he receives constant training to stay up to date with the mortgage industry changes. Pinnacle is a direct lender so they have their own resources to underwrite and fund loans to a wide diversity of customers. Pinnacle provides a lot of resources and honest advice to their loan officers and their customers. It's for that reason that Pinnacle has received in 2006 the Seal of Approval as the nation's most ethical lender by Consumer Advocate Harj Gill's. Adrian has always enjoyed working with top quality organizations and professionals, such as his mentor and broker, Marcelo Parada, from the Annandale office in Virginia. They work as a team to help the education and lending process go as stress less as possible.

FinANciNq

"Neither a borrower nor a lender be; for loan oft loses both itself and friend, and borrowing dulls the edge of husbandry."
—Lord Polonius (Shakespeare's Hamlet, 1603)

DEFINITIONS

FinANciNq is AN iNTEGRAl pART of the purchase and sale of real estate. Even institutional and corporate buyers of real estate use borrowed money to buy real estate. This chapter explains how to utilize real estate financing in the most effective and profitable way possible, focusing on investors. But these techniques are also applicable to potential homeowners. There are only two formulas to understand: one is the Return on Investment (ROI) and the other is how to calculate the monthly payment.

In finance, like many things in life, there are two sides of the coin. On one side is the lender, and on the other side is the borrower, the coin being the property itself, whether it's land, a single family home, an apartment building or a commercial property. Few people or investors have the funds to purchase properties for all cash, and those who do, they are very careful to diversify their portfolio. There are a couple of cases where cash may be a better choice for purchasing a property: when you want to close super quick or when you want to invest long term with some retirement money.

A lender is someone who has access to money and is willing to take a risk and lend it to a borrower for a fee, called interest, for a specific time period and for a specific payment amount or repayment rules (in the case of adjustable rate mortgages.) Their motivation is to make a profit for themselves or their investors. To stay in business and avoid becoming a charity, lenders have to manage risk, most of the time collecting additional insurance from the borrower or asking for more collateral. Lenders can be: the current property owner (owner financing,) a single investor, a small group of investors incorporated or in a legal partnership, mortgage companies of different sizes, a Real Estate Trust, institutional investors, etc.

On the other side, a borrower is someone who needs money to purchase (or sometimes lease) a property to live or invest. For investors, some of the strategic options are: wait—and let inflation or appreciation do its trick, improve or remodel to sell at a profit, or rent with or without option to buy. Each of those strategies requires different financing options because they have different time and risk parameters. The borrower is willing to pay money for "the privilege" of borrowing money. It is paid upfront as loan points or regularly as interest.

A borrower can be a simple homeowner who will use the property for personal enjoyment or an investor, who will not live in the property, but will expect to make a profit by renting or eventually selling his or her rights to the property. Is not uncommon for many speculator-investors to buy new homes at pre-construction prices and sell their right to the property when the neighborhood is fully developed and the perceived value has increased, netting about 5 to 15% of the property value for their initial investment. If you have ever seen those "for sale" signs when a new development neighborhood was about to be complete and thought that the current owner may have made a mistake, they you were the one mistaken.

An investor usually will estimate if the deal is worthy of his or her time by calculating the Return on Investment (ROI) as follows: take the annual cash flow or income and divide it by the annual operating expenses. In the case of an investment property, take the equity increase and divide it by the amount of cash invested or down payment. Then, based on this number and his or her own criteria (or the investor's guidelines) they will decide whether to pursue the deal or not. If the ROI is going to be less than 5%, you might as well park the money on a Certificate of Deposit (CD) and forget about investing on that deal. A shrewd investor plays it safe and avoids taking unnecessary risks.

ROI example 1: you purchase a house using all of your cash for $200,000. If the property were to increase in value 10% over 12 months, it would now be worth $220,000. Your ROI would be 10%. Even if you rent the house and profit an additional $20,000 (to which you still have to deduct mortgage expense, taxes and depreciation,) your maximum ROI in this cash purchase is about 20%. Another factor to consider: while real estate values may increase, an all-cash purchase may not be economically feasible because the investor's cash may be utilized in more effective ways.

ROI example 2: armed with the proper financing, you purchase a house using $20,000 of your own cash and $180,000 in borrowed money, a 10% increase in value would still result in $20,000 of increased equity, but your return on your cash is 100%! The investor's plan is to rent the house to off-set the interest expense of the loan. If the investor wanted to use all avail-able cash, with 20% down payments, the investor could have purchased five houses of $200,000 which in one year, for the same 10% appreciation, could be worth $1,100,000. In this last case the ROI would be 50%. Since there are five houses involved, the potential earnings could be higher, and so are the potential loses. There is always risk involved.

Question: How come I get this flyer or I see an advertised rate but after I get a quote from my broker or loan officer, the rate is usually higher?

Answer: first of all, NEVER believe those teaser rates! They are designed to get your attention and make a call to satisfy your curiosity (it worked, didn't it?). There are several factors that determine your interest rate:

1. Current index rate for the product you are applying for: fixed rate, variable rate or a combination of both (hybrid.) We'll discuss Adjustable Rate Mortgages (ARMs) in next question.

2. Your personal, joint or corporate credit score discussed in more detail in chapter 8,

3. The Loan to Value (LTV) ratio is the percentage calculated as the amount of the loan divided by the appraised value of the property. The preferred LTV is 80% because that's what many government programs require. The LTV is basically a number that represents what risk the lender is going to cover, which will affect your rate. Example 1: if you want to borrow 95% of a property valued at

$200,000 (95% LTV), you are risking $10,000 but the lender is risking $190,000. Example 2: same property, but now you put down 30% or $60,000 (70% LTV.) Your lender is now risking less ($140,000) and is willing to give you a discount on the rate of at least 0.25%

4. Term of the loan, usually 15, 20, 30 or 40 years. The longer it takes to repay the loan, the higher the rate since that increases the risk for the lender.

5. Loan specific adjustors: there are a few items that can affect the final rate of the loan, but those vary from lender to lender and you have to ask to get them, so don't be afraid to ask! A measly 0.125% in a rate discount can add up to a few thousand in the life of the loan. Here are a few adjustors: Cash-out refinance+, Second or investment home+, excellent FICO-, low LTV-, loan size (jumbo loans or very small loans pay extra!) interest only+.

Question: one of my friends could not buy a house because his appraisal came too low, even though he was pre-qualified.

Answer: the appraisal is the final word to the bank about how much risk they are willing to take when lending you money. If real estate values decrease or expectations were too high, the most recent appraised value may not match what the borrower (or seller) had in mind, in which case is best to walk out of the deal. Pre-qualifying a person is just that, "before purchase". Many things can happen before the purchase is complete, like spending on a new car which will change the total debt to income ratio.

Question: what is an ARM? What are the problems with it?

Answer: adjustable-rate mortgage (ARM), are dozens of mortgage variations to suit the lender's profit motives and borrower's needs. It is basically a mortgage that is not fixed, but there some rules: ARMs have two limits, or caps, on the rate increase. One cap regulates the limit on interest rate increases over the life of the loan; the other limits the amount the interest rate can be increased at a time.

For example, if the initial rate is 6 percent, it may have a lifetime cap of 11 percent and a one-time cap of 2 percent. The adjustments are made monthly, every six months, once a year, or once every few years, depending on the "index" on which the ARM is based on. An index is an outside public reference source such as the following: • LIBOR (London Interbank Offered Rate)—based on the interest rate at which international banks lend and borrow funds in the London Interbank market.

- COFI (Cost of Funds Index)—based on the 11th District's Federal Home Loan Bank of San Francisco. These loans often adjust on a monthly basis!

- T-bills Index—based on average rates the Federal government pays on U.S. treasury bills, also known as the Treasury Constant Maturity, or TCM.

- CD Index (certificate of deposit)—based on average rates banks are paying on six-month CDs.

ARMs can be very risky because of the uncertainty of future interest rates, but they can be used effectively with a little common sense. If you plan to sell or refinance the property within a few years, then an ARM may make sense. You may have to review your short-term and long-term goals with your lender before choosing an index.

INTEREST RATE CHART -
MONTHLY PAYMENT PER $1,000 BORROWED

Interest Rate %	Term 15 Year	Term 30 year	Interest Rate %	Term 15 Year	Term 30 year
4	7.40	4.77	7 5/8	9.34	7.08
4 1/8	7.46	4.85	7 3/4	9.41	7.16
4 1/4	7.52	4.92	7 7/8	9.48	7.25
4 3/8	7.59	4.99	8	9.56	7.34
4 1/2	7.65	5.07	8 1/8	9.63	7.42
4 5/8	7.71	5.14	8 1/4	9.70	7.51
4 3/4	7.78	5.22	8 3/8	9.77	7.60
4 7/8	7.84	5.29	8 1/2	9.85	7.69
5	7.91	5.37	8 5/8	9.92	7.78
5 1/8	7.97	5.44	8 3/4	9.99	7.87
5 1/4	8.04	5.52	8 7/8	10.07	7.96
5 3/8	8.10	5.60	9	10.14	8.05
5 1/2	8.17	5.68	9 1/8	10.22	8.14
5 5/8	8.24	5.76	9 1/4	10.29	8.23
5 3/4	8.30	5.84	9 3/8	10.37	8.32
5 7/8	8.37	5.92	9 1/2	10.44	8.41
6	8.44	6.00	9 5/8	10.52	8.50
6 1/8	8.51	6.08	9 3/4	10.59	8.59
6 1/4	8.57	6.16	9 7/8	10.67	8.68
6 3/8	8.64	6.24	10	10.75	8.77
6 1/2	8.71	6.32	10 1/8	10.82	8.87
6 5/8	8.78	6.40	10 1/4	10.90	8.96
6 3/4	8.85	6.48	10 3/8	10.98	9.05
6 7/8	8.92	6.57	10 1/2	11.05	9.15
7	8.99	6.65	10 5/8	11.13	9.24
7 1/8	9.06	6.74	10 3/4	11.21	9.33
7 1/4	9.13	6.82	10 7/8	11.29	9.43
7 3/8	9.20	6.91	11	11.36	9.52
7 1/2	9.27	6.99			

Rate chart example: $250,000 loan at 8% amortized over 30 years.
Annual payment per $1,000 is $7.34; so 250 × 7.34 = $1,834.41 per month.

If you are using a personal computer or Personal Digital Assistant, Microsoft Excel has a built-in function to calculate monthly payment, called PMT, which calculates the payment for fixed rate loans. Be aware that the interest rate has to be entered as a monthly decimal, so to calculate the monthly payment of a 30 year $500,000 loan at 6% annual interest you would enter: =PMT(0.06/12,360,500000), then click OK or press [Enter] and you will see the result displayed as $2,997.75. This Payment is for Principal and Interest only and does not include Taxes and Insurance or any other fees.

The principal is a portion of the original amount borrowed, distributed across the term of loan. The payments made near the beginning of the loan are mostly interest, while the payments near the end are mostly principal. Lenders increase their return and reduce their risk by having most of the profit (interest) built into the front of the loan. Another way they lock you in is by having prepayment penalties, like up to six months of interest. Be aware! Ask in advance, when discussing with your loan officer, and before you sign any papers, if the mortgage carries any prepayment penalty. Competitive lenders will not include penalty, but smaller ones can lock you for one or two years.

The interest only mortgage is basically a simple interest loan, whereby the principal is not repaid until the end of the loan. Example: A $200,000 loan at 12% simple interest is $24,000 per year, or $2,000 per month. To calculate monthly simple interest payments, take the loan amount (principal), multiply it by the interest rate, and then divide by 12. In this example:

$200,000 × .12 = $24,000 per year ÷ 12 = $2,000 per month.

On the average mortgage, on the first 10 years you only pay about 10% of the principal anyway. If you are planning to invest in a house for less than 10 years, interest only payments may be a way to go. If you are a homeowner and you know that property values are going up in value for your area, it may be worth considering an interest only mortgage, since most would still let you send in an extra payment (or whatever you can afford) towards the principal.

The next two items usually included with your payment are: Taxes and Insurance. The monthly portion of the payment accumulates into an escrow account at your lending institution it gets disbursed from there to your state or county and to your insurance company at the appropriate times in the year. Depending on your financial situation, you can elect to pay the taxes and insurance yourself rather than through an escrow account. Many lenders will let you do it this way for a fee, since they are losing the interest on the escrow and it increases their risk.

So now you have the complete picture of the monthly payment or PITI = Principal + Interest + Taxes + Insurance and you should be able to calculate it from the price of the property.

The insurance above refers to the regular homeowner liability insurance. There is an additional insurance that certain borrowers pay when they cannot meet the loan guidelines, specifically the Loan To Value (LTV.) This insurance has many names, but it is one form or another of Private Mortgage Insurance (PMI.) As an investor, you should plan your financial deals to avoid having to pay unnecessary insurance or additional fees.

PRODUCTS

Because financing plays a large part in real estate sales, it also affects values; the higher the interest rate, the larger your monthly payment. On the other hand, the lower the interest rate, the lower the monthly payment. Thus, the lower the interest rate, the larger the mortgage loan you can afford to pay. Therefore, the larger the mortgage you can afford, the more the seller can ask for in the sales price. Because most buyers borrow most of the purchase price, the prices of houses are affected by financing. Thus, when interest rates are low, housing prices tend to increase, because people can afford a higher monthly payment. Conversely, when interest rates are higher, people cannot afford as much a payment, generally driving real estate prices down, which has been the situation in most markets for most of 2006.

In difficult markets (high prices, high demand, or high interest rates) lenders start introducing new products so more buyers or investors can qualify, otherwise there won't be any sales. Adjustable Rate Mortgages or Interest Only mortgages with an initial low rate are popular once again because it is easier to qualify when taking into account.

The mortgage industry is always changing and producing new types of products in order to make buying a house a reality for many and making it easy to buy for the investor. In some markets, if lenders were using the old rule of three times your annual income as a maximum qualifying amount, they would go out of business very soon. Some old fashioned investors have as a goal to own their houses free and clear. For other investors, they would rather put their money to work in more houses and they would prefer to pay as little as possible per month in order to generate a positive cash flow.

For that reason, new families of mortgage products like the 40 year old mortgage or the "Interest Only" mortgage have become available.

Another new product is the "Hybrid ARM" which is an ARM that is fixed for a period of three, five, or even seven years. After that time, the rate will adjust, usually once (hence the expression "3/1 ARM" or "5/1 ARM") and then remain fixed for the term of the loan. The initial rates on these loans are not as good as a six-month ARM but will give you more flexibility and certainty (generally, the longer the rate is fixed for, the higher interest rate you'll pay).

Conventional versus Non-Conventional Loans:

Conventional financing is when a private commercial lender provides the money. Non-conventional loans are insured or guaranteed by the federal government.

Government Mortgages

Insured against default by the Federal Government, making qualification less stringent:

- FHA loans are insured by the Federal Housing Administration. FHA loans require 3% down payments and are 15 and 30 year fixed rate loans or 1 year ARMs.
- VA loans are guaranteed by the Department of Veteran Affairs. VA loans are only available to eligible veterans or surviving spouses of deceased veterans.

No down payment required! Up to 100% financing allowed. Maximum loan amounts for government loans are set geographically. Mortgage refinancing into government loans is only available to existing holders of government mortgages.

Conforming Loans

Conventional loans are generally broken into two categories: conforming and nonconforming. A conforming loan is one that conforms or adheres to strict Fannie Mae/Freddie Mac loan underwriting guidelines.

- They feature 0% to 20% down payment options.

- Usually fixed mortgage rates for 15 to 30 years or ARMs.

- Maximum conforming limit is $417,000.

Conforming loans are a low risk to the lender, so they offer the lowest interest rates. Conforming loans also have the strictest underwriting guidelines.

1. Borrower must have a **minimum of debt**. Lenders look at the ratio of your monthly debt to income. Your regular monthly expenses (including mortgage payments, property taxes, insurance) should total no more than 25 percent to 28 percent of your gross monthly income ("front-end ratio"). Additionally, your monthly expenses plus other long-term debt payments should total no more than 36 percent of your gross monthly income ("back-end ratio").

2. **Good credit rating**. You must be current on payments. Lenders will also require a certain minimum FICO credit score

3. **Funds to close**. You must have the requisite down payment (generally 20 percent of the purchase price, although lenders often bend this rule), proof of where it came from, and about 3 to 6 months of cash reserves in the bank.

Non-conforming loans:

Non-conforming loans are loans that cannot be processed by conforming guidelines, because of lack of funds, documentation, good credit, etc. So they represent a higher risk to the lender, which will be translated as a consequence, into a higher interest rate for the borrower. Non-conforming loans have no set guidelines and vary widely from lender to lender. In fact, lenders often change their own non-conforming guidelines from month to month.

Non-conforming loans are also known as "sub-prime" loans, because the target customer (borrower) has credit and/or income verification that is less-than-perfect. The sub-prime loans are often rated according to the creditworthiness of the borrower – "A", "B", "C" and "D."

The sub-prime loan business has grown enormously over the past ten years, particularly in the refinance business and with investor loans. Every lender has its own criteria for sub-prime loans, so it is impossible to list every loan program available on the market.

As you read so far, investors use mortgage loans to increase their leverage. The more money an investor can borrow, the more he or she can leverage the investment. Rarely do investors use all cash to purchase properties, and when they do, it is on a short-term basis. They usually refinance the property after renovations to get their cash back or sell the property for cash. For many investors, zero or no money down may be a goal, but it limits their options when buying. You can get two mortgages for 80/20 of the property value and settle with no money down.

The challenge is that loans for investors are treated as high-risk by lenders when compared to owner-occupied properties loans. Lenders often look at leveraged investments as risky and are less willing to loan money to investors. Lenders assume (often correctly) that the less of your own money you have invested, the more likely you will be to walk away from a bad property. In addition, fewer investor loan programs mean less competition in the industry, which leads to higher loan costs for the investor. The goal of the investor thus is to put forth as little cash as possible, pay the least amount in loan costs and interest, while keeping personal risk at a minimum.

LENDERS

As we mentioned earlier, there are many sources of money. Most investors prefer to deal directly with a mortgage broker. The broker is a middleperson; he does the loan shopping and analysis for the borrower and puts the lender and borrower together.

As the lending products change and new regulations come in effect, is very important to trust a competent mortgage broker to help you in your investments, like a tax professional or attorney can help you in their areas of expertise. So we strongly recommend that you consider consulting with an experienced mortgage broker or loan officer in order to understand what the best deal is for you based on your investment goals.

Just like when you interview a professional services firm, when selecting a loan officer or lending company you need to keep this factors in mind:

Length of Time in Business: Because the mortgage brokering business is not highly regulated in most states, there are a lot of fly-by-night operations. Many mortgage brokers will bait you with "too good to be true" loan programs that most investors won't qualify for. It is the old bait and switch trick!

Company Size: A big company can also have high employee turn-around, or you may get the run around a lot. If you are dealing directly with a broker, it is often a one-person operation, which may be hard to get to all the time. A small to midsized company is a good bet. You will be able to get the boss on the phone, but he or she will have a good support staff to handle the minor details.

Experience in Investment Properties: It is important to deal with a mortgage broker or banker that has experience with investor loans. Owner-occupant loans are entirely different than investor loans. And, it is important that the broker or lender you are dealing with has a number of different programs.

Internet based companies: while there is a lot of information out there, virtual companies are very risky. Many highly advertised Web sites offer "teaser rates" to get your name and phone and they will send your loan request information to a dozen companies since they are in the referral business! They usually have a narrow product selection since they deal mostly with consumers.

Six Questions to Ask Your Lender

1. How many regular investor clients do you have?

2. Do you get any back-end fees from the lender?

3. What percentage of your loans don't get funded?

4. What kind of special loan programs do you have for investors?

5. What income and credit requirements do I need?

6. What documentation will I need to supply you with?

The other way to find qualified mortgage brokers or investors that know them is by attending your local Real Estate investors group. Here in Northern Virginia there are two well known and well attended groups:

- The Real Estate Community Networking Group www.realestatecng.com

- DC/VAREIG — fastest growing real estate investing club www.dcvareig.com/

Many of these investor's groups meetings offer real networking and learning opportunities for most investors. Check on the National Real Estate Investors Association (REIA) web site, www.nationalreia.com, for a group near you, or start your own!

CONTACT INFORMATION & ADDITIONAL RESOURCES:

You can contact him at **amikeliunas@pinnaclefinancial.com** or **Adrian@Mikeliunas.com.**

CHAPTER 08

CREDIT POWER:
The Heavily Guarded Secrets of the Banking Industry

by JOHN DECKYS

John Deckys is a success story. From very humble beginnings on Chicago's South Side to having bought and sold millions in real estate, stocks and commodities, John brings us a wealth of experience. As an entrepreneur and a seasoned real estate and financial markets investor with over 20 years of experience, John is a wealth of information to his clients, brings great depth to his presentations and is a frequently requested public speaker. His areas of expertise include credit, real estate finance, real estate portfolio development, investing and wealth accumulation, Federal Reserve policy and interest rates, macro economic research, and independent business ownership & development. John has a bachelor's degree in economics from Loyola University of Chicago with additional concentrations in accounting and finance and also holds an Honorary Doctorate from the "School of Hard Knocks".

Personally, John lives in Colorado with his wife, Christy, three very active children and their cat Max. He enjoys all things Colorado and is also very active mentoring our youth. He currently sits as an Advisory Board Member of the Monarch High School Future Business Leaders of America (FBLA), serves on the FBLA scholarship committee, has been an FBLA state competition judge and has presented at their national convention. John also guest lectures at high schools, colleges, businesses and various associations on a variety of business related and wealth accumulation topics.

CREDIT POWER:
The Heavily Guarded Secrets
of the Banking Industry

Your credit score is your life's financial report card. As
a consumer and especially as a real estate investor knowing how to build,
maintain, and maximize your credit score is critical. Credit impacts virtually every facet of our lives and having great credit can save you hundreds of
thousands of dollars as a real estate investor. Your credit score will not only
affect your mortgage rates and credit card rates it will also affect your auto
loan rates, your auto insurance rates, your home insurance rates, and even
your job prospects.

In this chapter, I have so much I want to tell you, but only 5,000 words
to do it in. So, rather than bog you down with interesting but not very applicable information, I will do a brief overview of credit and then we are going
to get right into the meat and potatoes of the credit scoring model and how
you can build, manage, and manipulate your FICO score.

So, what is the big deal about credit? Quite simply, credit is not only
a deal maker, it is also a hidden wealth builder. To have great credit you
must manage your finances properly and make sound financial decisions. The
byproduct of these sound financial decisions is greater wealth accumulation
through tremendous payment savings over time and the ability to do significantly more transactions.

Credit as defined by Webster's dictionary is a belief or trust that one
will pay later. Your credit score is a snapshot of your credit risk at a specific
point in time and gives a creditor/underwriter a fast objective measurement
that quantifies the likelihood that you will pay your bills without being over
90 days late. The bottom line is credit scores establish a percentage of risk that
might be involved in a loan. Your credit scores are commonly known as your
FICO scores because they are generated by a mathematical model built by
the Fair Isaac Company. FICO scores range from 300 to 850. Excellent credit
is anything over 720. That is our goal. The three credit bureaus are Equifax,
Trans Union and Experian and all three use the same FICO scoring model.

The Fair Credit Reporting Act passed in 1971 by Congress established guidelines for fair practices in the use of credit scoring. The Fair and Accurate Credit Transactions Act of 2003 was passed to further protect American's and improve consumer credit awareness. You can get 1 free credit report from the bureaus every 12 months at www.annualcreditreport.com.

THE 5 VARIABLES OF THE FICO SCORING MODEL

Now, let's get to the meat and potatoes of credit. The following are the five variables that determine your FICO score along with the percentage impact that each variable has on your score.

PAYMENT HISTORY: 35%

With a 35% impact to your FICO score this has the greatest impact. Anything other than paying on time will have a negative impact. Paying on time means that your bill is paid within 30 days of the due date. Missing a high payment has a greater impact than missing a low one. Missing a mortgage payment has the greatest impact. So, if you must miss a payment miss anything but your mortgage payments. Additionally, delinquencies in the last two years carry more weight than others.

How important is payment history? The following example will illustrate. A client of mine who earns $1.2 million annually and had $7 million liquid in the bank and also had a 710 FICO score, co- signed on a mortgage for his daughter. She was over 30 days late on one mortgage payment in the last 12 months and this prevented him from getting the best financing available in the marketplace. Sure, he was able to get a loan, but with his financial capacity and his inability to obtain the best rates in the country, it demonstrates the significant impact that payment history has on you're ability to get the best financing terms. So, pay your bills on time!

OUTSTANDING CREDIT BALANCES: 30%

With a 30% impact to your flight go score this has the next greatest impact. This is the ratio between your outstanding debt balances and you're available credit limits. So, if you have a credit card with a $10,000 credit limit, and a $5,000 balance on it, your ratio is 50%. A good ratio is anything below 50% of your available credit. Below 30% allows the scoring model to score you even stronger and keeping your balance as close to zero as possible or at zero, maximizes this variable's impact on your FICO score. Keep in mind that a ratio of 50% doesn't bring your score down its simply prevents it from going higher faster. However, once you max out a credit card your score is negatively impacted. If you go one dollar over your available credit limit the negative impact is doubled. So, it is better to have numerous credit cards with low balances and low ratios, than it is to have only a few cards with high balances and high ratios.

So, as investors, if you know you are going to need to establish additional credit to do more deals, it is in your favor to go out and get as much credit as possible before your currently available credit lines get max'd out.

Also, note that in the current market environment the ratios on credit cards have a much greater impact than they do on mortgages. Again, let me illustrate. A client came to me with a $150,000 home equity line of credit that was max'd out. He also had two additional credit cards, each with a $20,000 limit. The cards had $2,500 and $3,500 balances. We needed to increase his credit scores in order to obtain A paper financing. Through a wonderful credit score simulation model, we did the following analysis. We paid off the entire $150,000 line of credit and the model showed a four-point increase in the credit score. We then paid off the two credit cards whose ratios were extremely low, and not the $150,000 HELOC, and the model showed a 24 point increase in the credit score. As this illustrates, in the current market environment credit cards can have a nasty impact on scores and must be managed very diligently.

Keep in mind that the credit scoring model is developed around several statistical methods which makes it very dynamic and allows scores to be impacted based on current consumer behavior and payment patterns. It also divides borrowers into high and low default risk classes and estimates the probability of default based on historical data on loan performance and the credit characteristics of the borrower. Additionally, through artificial intelligence algorithms, credit models can now allow for some learning through experience to discern the relationship between borrower characteristics and the probability of default. The bottom line is they are watching everything we do financially and how we do it, and using it to assess our default risk. Currently, consumers with credit card balances are showing a much greater likelihood of default than in the past. As the previous example illustrates, having even small credit card balances at this time can dramatically impact your scores. So, manage your credit card debt carefully! Again, it is better to have more credit cards with lower balances than fewer credit cards with higher balances. So, if your ratios seem to be an issue, either get additional credit cards or call your current creditors and asked them to increase your current credit limits.

CREDIT HISTORY: 15%

Credit history has a 15% impact on your credit score and it is the length of time since a credit line was established. The longer your credit history is, the greater the impact to your score. Typically, a two-year credit history is needed to have relatively strong credit and the ability to maintain a higher FICO score. The scoring model puts most weight on the current three years of credit history. The most recent 12 months has the greatest impact, months 13 through 24 have the next greatest impact, and months 25 through 36 have the third greatest impact.

Most lenders have credit history and credit trade line minimum requirements. For example, a financial institution may require a minimum of three credit trade lines with payment activity within the last six months. One of the trade lines may need to have been open for a minimum of 24 months and have an available credit limit of at least $5,000. The other two required credit trade lines may need to have been active for at least 12 months but with possibly know minimum credit limit required. All financial institutions will have different requirements, however, just know that there are minimum credit requirements in order to get the best financing available. So, if you have limited credit, get more and be sure to ask your lender if they have minimum credit requirements beyond the credit scores.

Be aware that if you feel the need to cancel a few existing credit cards, you want to cancel the newest cards with the shortest trade history. You never want to cancel a card that has a long trade history because not only will you lose the trade history scoring, which is a 15% impact, but, over time, you will also lose the 35% impact from your payment history, as well as, the 30% impact from your debt to available credit ratio. Ouch!

TYPE OF CREDIT: 10%

Type of credit has a 10% impact on your credit score. What the model is looking for here is a portfolio of different types of credit to see that you can manage a variety of different types of credit obligations properly. An example of a diversified credit portfolio is one that would include mortgage loans, installment loans, and credit cards. Keep in mind that you do not have to have a varied portfolio of credit to obtain a high FICO score, it simply gives you the best opportunity to obtain the strongest possible credit rating that you can. A diverse credit portfolio is also a significant benefit when something does happen to our credit, like a late payment. A diversified credit portfolio will minimize the negative impact of the late payment because of the overall strength it gives our credit.

INQUIRIES: 10%

Inquiries are the fifth and final variable that impact credit scores and they have a 10% impact. There are two types of inquiries, Hard Inquiries and Soft Inquiries.

Hard inquiries are any inquiries made by a creditor or lending institution in which the intent is to extend an individual additional credit. Hard inquiries MAY impact your scores. Any hard inquiries made within the last 12 months can affect your score. Also, be aware that these inquiries will show on your credit for 24 months. This gives an underwriter the ability to see how aggressive and individual may be in their pursuit of credit and gives the underwriter a little better insight into their finances. Depending on an individual's overall credit history and strength, each hard inquiry can cost from 2 to 50 points or more. The maximum number of hard inquiries that will reduce a score is 10 within the most recent six-month period.

Now most people do shop in today's market, so, due to current consumer behavior they have made some adjustments to the scoring model. The model now has incorporated a few exceptions regarding hard inquiries. Currently all <u>mortgage and auto loan</u> inquiries occurring within the most current 30 days of the time a new credit score is generated are ignored by way of an "Inquiry Buffer." So, you can shop with multiple financial institutions and any inquiries made within the last 30 days will not affect your credit score, so long as the inquiries are made for <u>mortgage or auto loans only</u>.

After the first 30 day "Inquiry Buffer" all <u>mortgages and auto loans</u> inquiries are broken into 14 day periods. No matter how many inquiries have been done in each of those 14 day periods, they will only count as one hard inquiry inside each of those 14 day periods. So, you can shop around all you want for <u>mortgages or auto loans only</u> and it will not affect your score for the most current 30 days and after that the effect is nominal. However, do realize that if you have challenged or very little credit, any hard inquiry can have a larger impact to your score.

Soft inquiries are inquiries made by us when we check your own credit, by institutions that have already extended us credit or insurance coverage when they want to check up on us, or by a firm that wants to make us an offer to apply for additional credit from their institution. Soft inquiries DO NOT impact your credit score. Soft inquiries will only show on your personal consumer credit report, not the banks, and they will stay on your consumer report for six months.

All of the companies that send us these credit card offers in the mail have done soft inquiries to our file to see if we may qualify to have additional credit extended to us. Beware that these are by no means a guarantee that you will be extended the credit that they are offering. When you apply for these credit offerings with these institutions, they will then do a <u>hard inquiry</u> to your credit file in order to determine whether or not you actually do qualify for the credit terms that they have offered to you. This hard inquiry may impact your FICO score.

REASON CODES:

When you receive a copy of your credit report you will find reason codes associated with your report. There may be as many as five reason codes on your report. These codes are telling you the reasons that each credit bureau has for giving you their specific score. The codes are reported in order of their importance and are the factors with the <u>strongest negative impact</u> on your. So, the first reason code represents the factor with the strongest negative impact on your score. The second reason code represents the factor with the second strongest impact on your score, etc. etc.

This is extremely powerful information because it tells us exactly what we need to address in order to improve our FICO scores. For example, if one reason is "proportion of balances to credit limit is too high on bank revolving or all of the revolving accounts," then we know that we must pay down some of our outstanding debt. Another reason code may say that "length of time accounts have been established," this would tell us that we simply need to establish a longer credit history for our score to improve.

As investors, this is critical information because it allows us to strategically manage the way we use our credit. For example, if we know that we need a 680 score in order to do a certain deal and our score is currently 682 with a top reason code of "proportion of balances to credit limit is too high on bank revolving or other revolving accounts," then we know not to put one more dime on any of our current available credit until our deal is closed. Doing so would have a very high probability of compromising our current score and killing the deal. So, it's not enough to just be aware of your FICO scores, we must also be aware of the reasons why we have the scores that we do.

A QUICK OVERVIEW OF GOOD, CHALLENGED AND ALTERNATIVE CREDIT

Keep in mind that the following are general guidelines. Each and every credit report is unique to that individual, so, the impact of the five factors that affect one's credit score are never exactly the same for any two given people. That is why when looking to manage and manipulate one's credit and credit scores an individual analysis must be done to determine the specific strengths and weaknesses of one's unique credit file.

OVERVIEW OF GOOD CREDIT:

- A timely pay history on all accounts

- Balances on credit cards do not exceed more than 50%, or best case have a zero balance every month but maintain current payment activity

- There is activity on a variety of credit obligations (a mortgage, installment loan, 3 to 5 credit cards)

- Open accounts have at least a 24 month history

OVERVIEW OF CHALLENGED CREDIT:

- Greater than eight to 10 open trade lines.\

- There were payments made over 30 days late in the last 12 to 36 months

- There are less than three open trade lines or less than three are being actively used

- Open trade lines are less than 24 months old credit

- Credit card balances are greater than 50% of the available credit

OVERVIEW OF ALTERNATIVE CREDIT:

There may be times when we as investors, or possibly our lease option tenants, either lack sufficient credit or simply have no credit at all. In this case, there are some lending institutions that allow "Alternative Credit." Although this does not necessarily improve our credit scores, it does allow us to demonstrate sufficiently positive credit and enable us or our lease option tenants to get financing. The following are a few examples of alternative credit:

- 12 to 24 months of canceled rent checks

- A credit letter from a utility company(s) demonstrating timely payments for at least the last 12 months

- A credit letter from a phone or cell phone company demonstrating timely payments for at least the last 12 months

- A credit letter from a cable company demonstrating timely payment for at least the last 12 months

Here's a little bonus for you. A company called Rent Reporters will report rent payments to the credit reporting agencies (www.rentreporters.com). This allows someone to generate a credit score using their monthly rent payments!

WHAT NOT TO DO AND WHAT TO DO WHEN APPLYING FOR ADDITIONAL CREDIT:

The following are quick tips that should always be considered when _applying for additional credit._

1. DO NOT: CLOSE CREDIT CARD ACCOUNTS

- It will increase your debt to available credit ratio (30% impact).

- It will affect the length of your credit history by decreasing it (15% impact).

- If you must close out in account make sure it is a more recent account.

2. DO NOT: MAX OUT YOUR CREDIT CARDS

- It's the fastest way to bring your score down 50 to 100 points!

- Again, keep credit cards below 30% of their available limit (remember this when paying down credit card balances).

3. DO NOT: APPLY FOR ADDITIONAL CREDIT OF ANY KIND

- Most hard inquiries, except for mortgage or auto loans, will ding your credit.

- Remember that inquiries have a 10% impact on your score.

4. DO NOT: DO ANYTHING THAT WILL RED FLAG YOUR FILE IN THE SCORING SYSTEM

If the scoring system sees any type of *unusual activity* in your file it may negatively impact your score until the model can determine what is taking place. So…

- Do not add new accounts.

- Do not co-sign on a loan.

(Co-signing on a loan will show up on your credit, plus, it obligates you to 100% of the indebtedness. This increases your debt ratios and can cost you deals if you are already pushing the high end of these ratios. Additionally, if they miss a payment it goes on your credit as well).

- Do not even change your name or address with the credit bureaus. The less "out-of-the-box" activity the better.

5. DO: STAY CURRENT ON EXISTINGING ACCOUNTS

- Pay your bills on time! (remember, it's a 35% impact!).

- One 30 day late can cost 30 to 75 points or more.

6. DO: CONTINUE TO USE YOUR CREDIT AS NORMAL

- Changing your spending patterns can affect your scores.

7. DO: CALL YOUR BANK OR BROKER FOR ADVICE

This assumes you are working with a competent source in regards to the credit scoring model (or contact my office at 720-329-2608 or email johndeckys@ earthlink.net).

- If you receive something from a creditor and are unsure of its ramifications.

- If you receive something from a collection agency.

- If you receive any financial document and are unsure of its ramifications.

TIPS ON AND MANAGING, MANIPULATING AND IMPROVING CREDIT SCORES

"The Greatest Impact Strategy"

Tips one through eight are ways to quickly impact your credit score. I call them "The Greatest Impact Strategy," and they are the techniques that you can use to quickly manipulate and/or maximize your credit scores. Tips nine through eleven can also have a significant impact, so, do not disregard them or discount their importance.

1. DO: DISTRIBUTE DEBT EVENLY AMONG CREDIT CARDS (QUICK IMPACT)

- This improves the ratio of outstanding debt to available credit (30% impact).

2. DO: RAISE CREDIT LIMITS (QUICK IMPACT)

- This improves the ratio of outstanding debt to available credit (30% impact).

- Always ask them to do this based on your credit history to avoid a hard inquiry.

They may still insist on doing a hard inquiry but it is worth asking.

3. DO: OPEN NEW ACCOUNTS TO TRANSFER BALANCES (QUICK IMPACT)

- Do this to lower your debt to available credit ratios (30% gain).

- You will receive a hard inquiry to open a new account (10% loss). The idea here is a lesser of two evils. We are taking a 10% negative impact to obtain a 30% positive one.

4. DO: BECOME AN AUTHORIZED USER (QUICK IMPACT)

- When you become an authorized user on someone else's credit card you obtain all the benefits of that card's payment history, debt to available credit ratio, and credit history. So, if someone has a 10 year old credit card with perfect credit you will receive all the benefits as if you yourself had had that card for 10 years.

5. DO: PAY DOWN ON ALL DEBTS ACROSS THE BOARD (QUICK IMPACT)

- Be aware of your debt to available credit ratios and pay down the cards with the higher ratios first. (you need some money to use this strategy).

7. DO: NEGOTIATE WITH YOUR CREDITORS: (QUICK IMPACT)

- If you have some funds available, you can negotiate discounted payoffs with your creditors (get everything in writing).

- If you receive a discounted payoff you will most likely be sent a 1099 at year end because the creditor will write off the discounted portion of the debt with the IRS and count it as income given to you. So, you will owe taxes on the discounted portion of the debt (a small price to pay to get significantly discounted payoffs).

8. DO: REMOVE INCORRECT NEGATIVE TRADE LINES: (QUICK IMPACT)

- It is not a problem to remove negative trade lines so long as you have the documentation verifying that the trade line is, in fact, incorrect.

- Send the documentation to each of the three credit bureaus.

9. DO: REPORT RENT TO THE CREDIT REPORTING AGENCIES:

- Rent payments can be reported to the CRAs (go to www.rentreporters.com). This does not have an immediate impact to one's credit, but, it is a fantastic way to build additional credit and it motivates tenants to pay their rent on time all the time!

10. DO NOT: CLOSE ACCOUNTS WITH A ZERO BALANCE:

- Closing an account with a zero balance will increase the debt to available credit ratio of your overall credit file (30% impact).

11. DO NOT: CONSOLIDATE TO 1 OR 2 CREDIT CARDS:

- Consolidating your debts to one or two credit cards will again increase your debt to available credit ratios on those individual cards (30% impact).

PUTTING IT ALL TOGETHER

So, we now know the five variables that make up our credit score. We've reviewed what to do and what not to do when we are applying for additional credit. We've, also, reviewed what to do and what not to do when managing or attempting to manipulate or maximize our credit scores. Now let's put it all together and review the order in which these tips and techniques should be implemented when attempting to repair, manipulate or improve our credit scores by way of "The Quickest and Greatest Impact Strategy."

HOW TO STEPS TO REPAIR, MANIPULATE AND IMPROVE CREDIT SCORES

STEP 1: REVIEW THE REASON CODES ON THE CREDIT REPORT:

- Remember these codes specify **the top reasons that your score was not higher.**

- Make note of their order of importance.

STEP 2: IDENTIFY AND VERIFY ALL THE TRADE LINES THAT MAY BE ASSOCIATED WITH EACH STATED REASON CODE:

- In most cases, unless every trade line in a credit file has a problem, every trade line in a credit file will not be associated with one of the stated reason codes.

STEP 3: STARTING WITH THE TOP REASON CODE AND ITS ASSOCIATED TRADELINES, BEGIN CORRECTING THE CREDIT REPORTS IN THE FOLLOWING ORDER:

1. Find **Negative** impact trade lines that are incorrect and have them removed.

2. Find **Positive** impact trade lines that are not reporting and have them added.

3. Find **Negative** trade lines that are correct and attempt to remove them.

An Example:

Let's say we have reviewed the reason codes and the top reason code affecting your credit score is "Proportion of balances to credit limits is too high on bank revolving or other revolving accounts" (STEP 1).

You would then locate all trade lines with a high debt to available credit ratio and verify that they are, in fact, yours (STEP 2).

If the trade lines are not yours they can be removed immediately (STEP 3, #1). If they are yours, then verify that the balances are being reported correctly. If the balances are not correct and are, in fact, lower, then have them corrected. This will bring down your debt to available credit ratio and have an immediate positive impact on your credit score. If the trade line and its balance is correct, then there isn't much you can do. You can either pay down on the balance or ask the creditor to increase your current credit limit. You go through this process for each reason code.

Upon reviewing the credit report you would also take note of any accounts that you might have where the "Proportion of balances to credit limits is NOT too high on bank revolving or other revolving accounts" and is NOT being reported to the credit bureaus. You would then call the creditor and ask them to report this trade line to the bureaus because it will have an immediate positive impact on your credit score by lowering your overall debt to available credit ratios (STEP 3, #2). Some creditors may not be willing to do this.

In our current example STEP 3, #3, does not apply. Realize, however, that negative trade lines that are correct are very hard to completely remove. If it is a legitimate debt and your rights according to the Fair Credit Reporting Act have not been violated and the statute of limitations on the debt has not expired, then your hands may be tied for awhile.

Wow, we have covered a ton of information and, yet, there is so much more I want to tell you. However, I am running out of my allotted chapter space, so, let me do a quick brain dump with some additional tips.

If you have no credit or completely trashed credit, you can establish new credit by getting secured credit cards. Just get on the internet and do a search for "secured credit cards" and you will get a list of banks that you can send a few hundred dollars to and they will issue you a credit card for the dollar amount that you sent them. If you did this with three or four banks you would immediately begin building new and perfect credit history quite rapidly.

If you need to repair items on your credit report and have all the proper documentation, I can do a rapid repair to your credit and have a new FICO score for you within three to five business days. Additionally, if you are just not sure of the best way to correct your credit, I have access to a FICO model simulator that gives specific recommendations on how to maximize your current credit score.

When dealing with creditors and credit reporting agencies always be nice! Keep a journal and include any contact person's name or operator number, always get things in writing, send all correspondence by certified mail with a return receipt requested, and always request a copy of your credit report once something is improved.

If you are serious about taking ownership of your credit and using it as a tool to maximize your investment capabilities and wealth, then go to www.thecreditseminar.com and register for one of my upcoming workshops. If you are now blown away by what you learn, I will simply refund 100% of your investment. It has been my experience in accumulating wealth in my lifetime that the more we learn, the more we earn, and that it is the books we read and the people we meet that allow us to grow and become bigger and better and wealthier than we are today.

Jim Rohn says it best, "Through testimonials and personal experience we have enough information to conclude that it is possible to design and live an extraordinary life." Great credit has played a major role in the creation of my wealth and in my ability to design and live my extraordinary life. That is my wish for you.

Feel free to contact me if you have any questions, would like additional information or need credit repair or mortgage assistance.

Best of Success,
John

CONTACT INFORMATION & ADDITIONAL RESOURCES:

John Deckys, Pres.
johndeckys@earthlink.net
720-212-0768 direct

Deckys Consulting, Inc.
www.deckysconsulting.com
"Empowering people with the knowledge and ability to create wealth"

UPCOMING SEMINARS:
www.thecreditseminar.com
www.themortgageseminar.com

FINANCE INFORMATION:
www.johndeckys.com
www.deckysconsulting.com

REAL ESTATE MYTHS AND MISCONCEPTIONS

by MARIA DAVIES

MARIA DAVIES STARTED INVESTING IN PROPERTY in 1990 and she freely admits that she's probably made every mistake in the book along the way. Her entire portfolio is located in the UK and comprises both residential and commercial real estate.

She attributes her lifestyle to her real estate investments and believes everyone should be involved, to some extent, in what she calls "the best investment in the world".

She has 2 successful UK limited companies, a US corporation, a large and ever-expanding property portfolio, a network marketing business and "works" at her favourite pastimes – real estate speaking and coaching women who want to invest.

REAL ESTATE MYTHS AND MISCONCEPTIONS

Talk TO ANYONE ABOUT PROPERTY INVESTMENT and they'll have at least some knowledge. But a little knowledge can be a dangerous thing, especially if it's "common" knowledge. What you'll often find is that much of this "common knowledge" consists of myths and misconceptions that have been perpetuated over the years. Perhaps some of these myths used to be true, but things change and you would do well to question every piece of advice you're given and reconsider everything you *think* you know on a regular basis.

Here are what I see as being today's top 10 myths and misconceptions around real estate with my thoughts on why you might want to reconsider each of them.

MYTH # 1 - LOOK FOR THAT ONE BIG DEAL

It sounds appealing to do the work once and gain big. Many investors dream of landing the Great White shark instead of bothering with the minnows. The problem is that if you lose control of the shark, he can eat you whereas a shoal of minnows won't. What the minnows will do, however, is feed you.

Of course I'm not talking about fish. I'm talking about doing one huge complex compared with many one bedroom apartment deals. If a one bedroom apartment goes wrong the chances are it won't break the bank, but if you sink everything into that one big deal and then it fails to work out, you could end up having to sell your home or even bankrupt yourself because you went for the big one.

The fact is that you can handle many minnows for the same effort you put into handling one shark. Whilst doing the small deals you'll be learning without risking everything. A big deal will throw you a big learning curve and may be exciting but there's calculated risk and there's folly. If you're not experienced enough to handle it or you don't have the financial backing as a safety net should things not work out, or if you only have one possible exit strategy, that's definitely folly.

It might take you longer, but if you chip away and build your investing muscles, you'll get to the big deal with the backing, contacts and knowledge you need to take a calculated risk.

MYTH # 2 - LOOK FOR THE NEXT BIG GROWTH AREA

If you're doing this just to get a kick start, that's great. We all want to find the best deal and get the quickest growth we can, so go ahead and research for the areas that will increase in value most quickly. The problem arises when you're *relying* on the quick growth so you can flip the property on, reselling it at a profit.

Now this can be done, particularly in a rising market and if you can get a *genuine* discount from the developer or seller, but what you have to remember is that this is speculating, not investing. I could tell you a great many horror stories of those who've come unstuck doing this.

So how can you protect yourself? By making sure that every deal you do has at least two exit strategies. If you're just buying with the idea that you'll flip it quickly to benefit from what you believe will be a quick increase in value, what happens if the market moves against you and the price drops. That's tough because once you're committed to buying the property, contractually; you have to buy it *at the price you've agreed*. The likelihood then is that you'll be unable to sell it at a profit and perhaps not even for the same price that you paid. In which case, you could be faced with taking a hit on the price and having to pay the difference.

If you know that the property would also rent out, should you end up having to keep it, for any reason, that's your second exit strategy. Just to let you into a little secret—I'm speaking from experience here because I also speculated on a deal that didn't quite work out due to the developer artificially inflating the prices of the properties. The problem was that while all investors, including, were trying to flip the properties, the developer then launched the rest of their properties in the complex at 20,000 less than we'd paid. This completely wiped out the discount and meant we had no chance of selling for what we'd paid for the properties.

How did it work out? Well I had to find 60,000 to complete the purchase, keep the apartment and rent it out at a loss each month. Of course, over time, the market will correct this mistake and my portfolio will recover. Fortunately, because I'm a player in the property market, I was able to raise the funds needed to complete the transaction and was able to cover the rental deficit from positive cash flow elsewhere in my portfolio. Can you imagine what a disaster this could be for someone who was unable to raise the funds or cover the mortgage payments? One deal like this could wipe them out. Don't let this happen to you!

MYTH # 3 - IF IT'S STICKING ON THE MARKET SOMETHING'S WRONG WITH IT

This is an example of a self-fulfilling prophecy. I've found some great deals from properties stuck on the market for a long time. Here's what happens:

- property is placed on the market but doesn't sell quickly;

- people notice it's sticking start speculating about why;

- seller wants to sell, has costs to cover so starts to reduce the price;

- now it's still on the market and the price is dropping which adds fuel to the speculation about what's wrong with it.

What's happening here is that everyone's following the herd mentality.

Recently, I bought a great place that had been on the market for over three years, unloved and unwanted. It's already paid for itself and I have plans in place that will bring me in over 33,000 plus an ongoing income.

I wonder how many people passed because they thought "there must be something wrong with it."

Never follow mob mentality because it's usually wrong. One of my strategies for locating a good deal is to approach agents and ask to see properties that have been on the market the longest. Then I find out as much as possible about the seller's situation and how motivated they are to sell. Usually, the longer the property has been stuck on the market, the more motivated the seller. The more motivated the seller, the more willing they may be to negotiation the price and other aspects of the deal to secure a sale.

MYTH # 4 - ONLY BUY PROPERTY YOU'D LIVE IN YOURSELF

I hear this all the time and it's just daft. Apart from the fact that when you look at a property to live in yourself, you get emotionally involved, that is the last thing you want to do in property investment. The best rentals are 1 & 2 bedroom flats close to transport. I live in a wing of a gorgeous 100+ year old mansion house in rural English countryside. There's no way I'm going back to a 1 or 2 bedroom flat, no matter how nice it is! Instead, get into the heads of your prospective tenants. If your tenant is a shift worker at the airport, what do they want?

- Black out blinds on the windows?

- Close to transport that runs 24/7?

- Safe to walk home in the early hours?

- Bedroom in the back away from street noise?

If your primary market is a shift worker with these requirements, he's not going to want your sweet family home beside a noisy school, even if it is the best school in the county. However, a family with young children at that school would snap it up.

Think "horses for courses" and beware of buying what suits YOU.

An additional comment, and a natural progression, is that you must also consider what your tenant wants when decorating and furnishing your property:

- Sharing students might want a work desk in each room and fast Internet connection;

- Professionals probably prefer a power shower to a bathtub;

- Families usually want a bathtub and somewhere to eat in the kitchen.

I'm sure you get the idea. Don't get emotionally involved in the décor and furnishings *you* like.

MYTH # 5 - YOU CAN SAVE MONEY BY DOING ALL THE WORK YOURSELF

How long will it take you to do the work? Let's say it takes you 2 months working part-time. Perhaps you saved yourself 1500 by doing this. But you lost 2 months' rent at 600, so you only really saved 300 and you spent your time doing this when it could have been better spent finding another great deal.

Two more considerations are "How professional a job can I do?" and "Would a professional do this more quickly than I will?" Better to pay a professional to get the work done quicker because time is money when it comes to property. Plus, a better quality job can increase value and yield a higher rent.

MYTH # 6 - ALL TRADESMEN ARE ROGUES

This is a topic of conversation that everyone will contribute to around the dinner table. We all have our stories of the plumber who took months to finish a job estimated to last two weeks, or the electrician whose excuses for not showing up get more creative by the day. It's easy to paint everyone with the same brush (assuming the painter shows up!), but most tradesmen are honest and intend to do a good job. Problems can arise for many reasons and you can do a lot to protect yourself and ensure your job goes smoothly and completes on time. Here are some tips:

- spec out the job from start to finish with as much detail as possible;

- put everything in writing with agreed price and start/finish dates;

- particularly mention of critical dates, e.g. times when certain aspects of the job must be completed;

- ensure both you and the tradesman sign both copies and give him a copy;

- ensure he knows how much it will cost you each day the job runs over and write into the contract that his fee will be reduced accordingly for every day's delay in completion (he will want some safeguard so he's not penalized if the job runs over through no fault of his, and this is only fair);

- ensure you agree the hours he will be on site, who will be responsible for providing the materials and the final fee for the job, fully detailed as to what the fee includes (NB: NEVER agree to a day rate unless you also get agreement as to the exact number of days the job will take);

- all businesses face cash flow problems so your tradesman will respond to you if you assure him you'll pay cash immediately on satisfactory completion;

- when the work is complete, arrange to fully inspect it with the tradesman present. If it's completed to your satisfaction, pay him then and there. If there's any work still to be done, agree a deadline to complete and arrange to meet again for a further inspection, letting him know you will be paying him cash on satisfactory completion;

- to get a job done more quickly, you could offer a bonus for early *satisfactory* completion;

- if the job is completed on time and you're happy, consider giving him an unannounced bonus anyway. He'll love you forever and you'll be a preferred client next time you call with a job.

In short, treat your workers with respect. You'll get a lot more out of them.

Myth # 7 - You have to sell to get your money out

When you sell property, you're killing the goose that lays the golden egg. At first glance it can seem attractive to sell to release funds because when you refinance a property you have to leave some equity—15%, perhaps, whereas if you sell, you get to take it all ... or do you?

Actually, no! First, you have marketing and legal costs to pay, and these can be considerable. If your property was previously rented and the rental income was covering the mortgage, you'll probably also have a period when the property is empty while it's on the market. If you have a mortgage, you'll still have to cover the payments. We all know how long it can take for a sale to be completed so be sure to factor in the mortgage payments for all these months, not to mention insurances, service charges and other running costs which must be covered by you during this void period. This can seriously dent your bottom line.

After the sale of an investment property, you still don't get to keep all the money either as you'll certainly have a tax bill on your profit if it's a profit worth having. Every country has different rules and you will have some allowances to take into account, but you will need to consider what proportion of your nice juicy profit goes straight to the taxman – ouch!

Finally, after taking your profit by selling, you're left with what? Nothing! No more income from that property and no more capital growth. Now if you want to get back into a position of income from property, you'll have to go out and buy another one, with all the associated buying costs involved in that, so you lose again. Is there a better way? You bet!

Do you realise that it's so much easier to raise finance on a property you *already own* rather than getting finance to buy initially?

Instead of selling, how about re-mortgaging the property? Contact a good broker and provide them with all the figures relating to your property. They'll need to know the following:

- current market value

- rental income

- existing mortgage amount

They will then tell you how much you could release from the property by refinancing with another lender.

A Quick Illustration

Here's an example of the sort of funds you might be able to raise by going through a refinance:

1. Property value:
    180,000

2. Existing mortgage:
    100,000

3. New mortgage at 15% of new value:
    153,000

4. New mortgage payments at 5% per annum (interest only):
    638/month

5. Rental required by lender at 125% of mortgage payments:
    798/month

This means that for an additional 220 a month, you can release 53,000 in one lump sum. If the rental income covers this payment, it's costing you nothing, so it's free money in your pocket!

Now let me just clarify a few points. First off, I've worked on a figure of a 5% interest rate on the new borrowing (4). Obviously, you will need to use the prevailing average rate at the time for wherever you are. There's every chance this rate could be lower than the 5% I've used, especially if you get a low fixed rate from a lender. Be careful, however, because when calculating the required rental figure (5), some lenders use their base rate rather than the rate you will actually be paying, which could be considerably less if you go for a good fixed rate. As a ballpark, go with the average or worst case scenario.

Another possible variable is the rental required figure (5). This is the figure by which the rent needs to cover the mortgage payments, e.g. if the lender requires 125% and your mortgage is 100 per month, your incoming rent needs to be 125 per month. Some lenders require a different figure—130%, for example. There are, however, lenders who don't necessarily need the rent to cover the payments at all. In this instance, they will want to see evidence that you, personally, could afford to cover any shortfall.

It's because there are so many options that I always recommend dealing with a good broker who will help you in identifying the best deal for you and in ensuring that you provide what's needed by the lender to get you quickly through the application process. When you find a good one, they're worth their weight in gold.

So after going through this process, we end up with 53,000 cash in our hand (less some costs and legal fees, and a possible early redemption payment on an existing mortgage, arrangement fees). PLUS we still have our 15% equity in the property (27,000 in this example), PLUS we still have a monthly income from the property, which might not be a huge amount but since, by this point, we've probably taken all our own money out, whatever we get becomes an infinite return on our investment as there's none of our original money left in the deal.

The advantages don't even stop there. We still own the property so we're still also benefiting from the growth in value over time. In a few years, we might want to take another lump sum out of this little cash cow as the value increases. But the best part is the lump sum of 53,000 you just released is TAX FREE money to you, in your hand. Why? Because you didn't sell the property, you didn't "realize the gain" so you don't create a tax liable event. In other words, the 53,000 is yours to spend as you please until such time as you decide to sell.

So what if you don't ever want to pay tax on the money? That's easy—don't ever sell. And why would you want to do that anyway because that would be killing the goose that will continue to lay the golden eggs for many years to come. Understand?

An author who puts this into great perspective is Andy Shaw whose book "Money For Nothing & Your Property For Free" is reviewed on my website at www.womeninpropertyinvestment.com.

The even easier alternative to this is to approach your existing mortgage lender for a further advance based on the increased value of the property. If you're a good customer (and sometimes even if you're not) your existing lender won't want to lose your business so I always make my current mortgage provider my first port of call for equity. People overlook this option, but it can be much easier since this provider already knows you *and* the property.

In fact, they frequently won't have to carry out a valuation. Instead, they will do a "desktop valuation" based on property market movements in the area. Hence you save on valuation fees, arrangement fees and legal fees. I've done this many times and had the additional funds in my bank account within about 10 days from my initial enquiry.

MYTH # 8 - YOU HAVE TO SWITCH LENDERS TO GET A BETTER MORTGAGE INTEREST RATE

Well, having just read the preceding advice in Myth # 7 you now know this simply isn't true. To save yourself time, grief and money, your first port of call should always be your existing lender for both release of additional funds AND to get a better interest rate.

Of course, there's no guarantee that your existing lender will be prepared or able to give you a rate that matches a very low loss-leading rate you might find on offer from a new lender, but there's no harm in trying. Here are some things to consider and some scripts you can use.

Find out whether you're locked in to an early redemption penalty if you switch lenders. Such a penalty might be a fixed sum, one month's interest or 3% - 5% of the sum originally borrowed. If you are locked into a penalty, don't just assume you have to wait until the early repayment period expires. If there are good fixed rates available now, and it looks like the base rate might be set to increase, it's small change to take the hit on the redemption penalty to get a lower ongoing payment (and possibly release a lump sum for further investment at the same time).

For example, I was coaching a lady very recently who wanted to begin her property portfolio. She told me she couldn't re-mortgage her home for another 7 months due to an early redemption penalty but she was desperate to raise funds for investment as well as having concerns about mortgage rates increasing, which looked likely at that point. This meant that by the time her redemption penalty ended, the fixed rates available to her would also have increased.

In her case, it turned out that the redemption penalty amounted to a little over 3,000, yet by getting a lower fixed rate immediately, she could release 27,000 and reduce her payments by just over 1,000 a year. If she waited, in order to save that 3,000, that excellent low fixed rate she just got would probably no longer be available. Of course the 3,000 was paid immediately out of the additional 27,000 released but even if she hadn't wanted to release additional funds, the monthly savings would have meant that it would be covered within the first year. Subsequent years on the low fix would then mean additional savings.

When you approach your existing lender, remember that they have to lend money to stay in business. It's what they do. If a lender doesn't lend money, they're not in business. You, on the other hand, do not have to borrow money, and you certainly don't have to borrow money from any one particularly lender. So it is you who is in control. The better your financial standing, the more in control you can be. This is why maintaining a good credit rating is one of the most important things for a property investor.

So when you approach a lender, always remember that you have a choice as to where you take your business. When you call your existing lender, therefore, you are offering them the chance to retain your business so you are doing them a big favour. Here's what you'll want to ask:

"I currently have a mortgage with you and I want to investigate obtaining a better rate/releasing funds. My broker has found me some very good fixed rates if I switch to another lender, but I'm quite happy with your company so I thought I would first find out what sort of deal you are prepared to offer to retain my business"

You might find that you'll be offered a variety of rates with different conditions attached. One of the conditions can be another tie-in with a redemption penalty if you redeem the mortgage early. Provided the redemption penalty only lasts the same length of the time as the fixed rate, don't be afraid of taking one of these deals if the rate is good. As soon as the fix ends, you can fix again -- possibly earlier, as we've already seen. And since you now know that you never want to sell, having a redemption penalty won't cause a problem in this regard either.

MYTH # 9 - PAY OFF YOUR MORTGAGE

Now why would you want to do a foolish thing like that? A mortgage is usually the cheapest form of borrowing you can find. You see, people have many misconceptions about loan money. Us mere mortals are taught that this is debt and that all debt is bad. But when people like Donald Trump and Robert Kiyosaki borrow money, they call it "gearing" and they'd rather invest this way than to use their own money. Not all debt is equal. Debt that you take to invest in appreciating assets is different from debt you *spend* on depreciating items. For a fuller explanation, I highly recommend the classic "Rich Dad, Poor Dad" by Robert Kiyosaki who labels such depreciating items "doodads."

If you pay money off your mortgage, what does that really do for you? Well, it just reduces or removes your mortgage payments and it might satisfy your need to stay within your comfort zone, but consider this... instead of using 150K to pay off your mortgage, how about using that money to place deposits on, say, 10 x 100K properties at 15K a property. Now you're got the capital growth on 10 properties valued at 100K, or 1 million in real estate (plus the one you originally owned). Even if your portfolio grows at 10% per annum, you're increasing your net worth by 100K per annum in the first year (and compounding year-on-year after that). This equates to 274 per day. Imagine waking up each day, stretching, and then remembering "Oh, I just made about 300 without even getting out of bed!" How good would that feel?

But now you're thinking "well that's all very well, but now I've got a debt that I didn't have before." True, but if those 10 properties are all rented out and bringing in an income over and above their own mortgage payments, the additional cash flow can be used to make the payments on the borrowing you've taken on your home mortgage.

So now you're thinking "yes but I don't want to be paying the mortgages forever, do I?" Don't you? Maybe and maybe not. If you've read through this chapter so far, you might now be starting to think that perhaps the line we've all been fed for years about paying off the mortgage as soon as we can isn't all it's cracked up to be. But some people still have a desire to eventually pay off the mortgage on their own home, which is a different prospect to paying off investment mortgages. If you feel you need to do this for your own comfort, you can.

Remember the growth on those 10 properties that we've now managed to buy by releasing mortgage money from our own home? Well now that you have a portfolio, which you might not have been able to buy *without* using the available equity in your own home, you have many more choices in life. As the investment properties increase in value, remember, you can re-mortgage them and take out additional borrowing – always assuming that the borrowing will be covered by the income they are achieving for you – and you can use these lump sums to pay off your home mortgage.

If, in spite of what I've already said, you want to pay off all your mortgages, as your portfolio value grows, you could sell some parts and use the profits to pay the capital gain AND the mortgages on other parts of your portfolio. If you're doing this, the best way is to do it piecemeal so you can benefit from your annual capital gains allowance.

Everyone's goals and circumstances are different so these are just ideas for you to consider. You have to do what's right for you, of course. Asset protection and inheritance issues should be considered pretty early on in your investing career.

MYTH # 10 - YOU CAN'T RELY ON PROPERTY TO PROVIDE FOR YOUR RETIREMENT

This old chestnut gets trotted out every time there's a discussion about the abysmal performance of personal pensions and my response is always "Why not?" After all, when you retire owning investment property, rents don't stop and nor does capital growth. In my area, property doubles in value every 6.7 years. What is the figure in your area?

This being the case, could you imagine buying just 1 property a year for the next 7 years? In the 8th year, go back to property number 1 & re-mortgage it because it's now doubled in value. Take that tax free mortgage money, stick it in the bank and live on it for the next 12 months. In year 9, go back to property number 2, which has now also doubled in value since you bought it 7 years earlier, and re-mortgage it, stick the tax free money in the bank and live on that for the next 12 months. So now it's year 10 and what are you going to do? You've got it – re-mortgage property number 3, which has doubled in value since you bought it 7 years ago. Now you have a tax free lump sum to bank and live on for the next 12 months, and so on until you've re-mortgaged all 7 properties in your portfolio.

Now what? Well, by now you've probably worked out that by year 14, property number 1, which we've left alone for the last 7 years has only gone and doubled in value all over again, so I guess we'll just have to go back and re-mortgage it again and take out another tax free lump sum. And I won't continue because it's getting boring now and I'm sure you've got the picture.

By the way, I'm often asked whether such lending is offered to people beyond retirement age and the fact is that it is. Remember, we are talking about investment finance which is based on the income potential of the properties, rather than a personal home mortgage which is based on your ability to pay.

Of course, this is over-simplifying the whole thing. Maybe in some years, you won't be able to re-mortgage a particular property, it's likely they will all appreciate at different rates and maybe in some years you'll be able to re-mortgage more than one and perhaps you'll want to re-mortgage them at different times because you can get a good interest rate at that particular time. But you also need to remember that rents also continue coming in, and the rental income on seven properties, even if they're only bringing in 50, 100, or 150 a month each after paying the mortgages, can make quite a difference to you in your retirement, in addition to the continuing capital growth.

CONTACT INFORMATION & ADDITIONAL RESOURCES:

Find out more at her website: **www.WomenInPropertyInvestment.com**

CHAPTER 10

REAL ESTATE INVESTMENT MISTAKES YOU MUST AVOID

by GARY TURNER

Successful investors look at life and opportunities different-ly. Success is not a subject taught in school, and if you want to learn it, there are two places to go: the school of hard knocks, which can be very painful and very expensive, or you can learn from someone who went to the school of hard knocks and lived to tell about it. I went to that school and the classroom is a mine field waiting to kill you. —Gary W. Turner

"The Future Belongs To Those Who Can Turn Their Dreams Into Reality"
        —Gary W. Turner

"I am a doctor turned real estate investor entrepreneur. I started investing in "pret-ty" homes. As the market shifts so does my investing style, and now I am forced to venture out into the world of "ugly" houses. I am fortunate enough to have Gary's friendship and mentoring behind me as valued experience as to avoid myself the school of hard knocks and save me hundreds of thousands of dollars in the process. Gary, thank you so much for all your insight, wisdom and guidance."
        —Dr. Amir Shalev

"Gary's real estate investing insights are a MUST READ for first time homebuy-ers and investors. If you are even thinking about buying property, read this now!"
        —Mark Smith - Real Estate Investor

"I first met Gary Turner in 2005 and found him to be one of the most knowledge-able and aggressive Real Estate Investors I had ever met. He is a real down to earth guy with a huge heart and a ton of real estate experience. I know Gary has helped a lot of people with their real estate investing, but his guidance has saved me literally hundreds of thousands of dollars! Thank you for your guidance and friendship."
—Robby LeBlanc - Investor/Musician, www.RobbyLeBlanc.com

"Gary is the best when it comes to envisioning the art of the deal for residential properties. His quick analysis of acquisition through exit strategy makes him a world class advisor to anyone who wants to make it as an investor in today's uncertain residential real estate market."
—Dr. Sandra Lilo - Real Estate Investor

"If you're tired of the late-night gurus who promise you fancy cars and island homes, then Gary is your real estate coach. You'll still get the fancy car, but you'll also get a healthy dose of reality. For the real deal in real estate, Gary's the best."
—Donna Fox – www.CreditMillionaire.com

"I met Gary early in his real estate career. As a fellow investor, both of us have seen the good and bad parts of the real estate cycles. What Gary has to offer, more than academic, is lessons learned that will help those reading avoid many costly mistakes. I highly recommend Gary's work and can vouch that Gary Turner is the "real thing.""
—Bruce Brady - Real Estate Investor

"As a seasoned real estate investor, I learned from the school of hard knocks. If I had had Gary's insight when I started, I could have saved literally hundreds of thousands of dollars. His knowledge and easy to understand practices are critical for any new or novice real estate investor. Pay attention!"
—Colleen Berg - Real Estate Investor

"Gary is the most down-to-earth, genuine and 'enterprising' individual I know. His information is not only realistic in the 'real world' of investing but relevant. Everybody should get this one!"
—Niki Curry - Real Estate Investor

"Gary Turner is to real estate what apples are to apple pie. His homespun, grass-roots knowledge of real estate is straightforward and easy to understand. I wish I would have had this information before I lost tens of thousands of dollars on the first two homes I bought and tried to sell. Since getting to know Gary and following his wisdom, we have successfully avoided the mistakes we made in our first two fiascos and purchased three other properties and have made substantial profits on each one. When it comes to real estate, Gary truly 'is the man'."

Gratefully,

Joel Brandley - Real Estate Investor

"Gary is an investor that has seen it all. He has a strategic perspective on everything, and I'm anxiously awaiting the release of his Real Estate Game-"Real Estate School of Hard Knocks".

—Elmie Litam - Real Estate Investor

A real estate investor since 1987, Gary presently owns over 50 properties acquired through a diversified real estate background which includes:

Single family residential
Fixer uppers and flips (online and offline)
Real estate auctions (online and offline)
Land development
Pre-foreclosures and foreclosures
Preconstruction of residential and condominiums
Bank, VA and HUD foreclosures

Prior to beginning a career in real estate, Gary worked in several different industries with significant experience in sales and facility management. Gary was a charter member of Mark Victor Hansen (co-author of *Chicken Soup for the Soul*) and Robert G. Allen's (author of *No Money Down*) Inner Circle. For 18 months this group met regularly to discuss real estate and personal/professional development. He is also an active member of Matt Bacak's "Big Boy Club".

MISTAKES AND SOLUTIONS

LONG TIME SUCCESSFUL REAL ESTATE INVESTOR, Gary W. Turner, shares a lifetime of knowledge and experience of critical real estate mistakes that you must avoid and provides you with simple solutions that can help you avoid these costly errors. Learning and practicing these simple strategies will prepare you to start harnessing the power of real estate to make your personal fortune - all without losing money through pitfalls that can set you back tens of thousands of dollars.

We've all heard *"People don't plan to fail; often they just fail to plan."* This is absolutely true in real estate, where a little planning will make all the difference in your investing career.

Beginning real estate investors are often an eager and determined lot. However, getting ahead of yourself in real estate investing can create mistakes, which can be very expensive lessons. Many seasoned investors have learned through trial and error to avoid these common mistakes. Make sure that these same problems aren't depriving you of the money you could be making right now and the future it could mean for you and your family!

1. Paying too much for a property: by over estimating value/under estimating repairs.

Making this mistake is often fatal for your investment property and sometimes for your real estate investing career. It is the hardest to recover from because you are starting off wrong from the get go. If your first investment property is an absolute disaster, it is very likely to be your first and last. It's very hard to climb back on the horse when your first ride ended with broken bones and a concussion. Investing too much money in a property is a common mistake that plagues many investors - especially beginning investors - but it is also a mistake that you can easily avoid with a few basic precautions. First, always do your research well. This means never buy a property unless you know exactly WHY you are buying it. When you first look at a property, quickly come up with the major advantages and disadvantages of the property. Make a solid list of all the property's liabilities. Does the property need repairs? What are the benefits and how do they stack up against the property's liabilities?

Always investigate the actual condition of the property and the neighborhood before you invest. The ideal property is an under priced piece of real estate that needs very minor repairs and cleaning, things you can do yourself or hire a handyman for, but is a property that is located in a desirable neighborhood (or in a community that is on its way up).

Some situations that may steer you toward paying too much are:

A. Getting into a bidding contest, either live on the courthouse steps or online on www.hud.gov or even on Ebay. You have found this cute little cottage house on the corner lot with beautiful flowerbeds and a nice neighborhood. It needs a little work and you just know it will be the perfect little house to fix-up and flip. It's being foreclosed on and you are just waiting for the morning it goes to the courthouse steps. The morning comes and you are there waiting. The steps have a lot of other people hanging around waiting also; surely they aren't all waiting for the house you came to bid on. Finally they call out the address you have been waiting on and suddenly there are six other people gathering with you. The bidding starts and only you and one other gentleman are bidding, you raise and he raises, then another bidder jumps in, and soon the price is over your estimate. Two more bids go in; you can't stand it so you raise the bid. The other gentlemen turn and look at you. They have reached their limit, and it's all yours. You suddenly realize you gave 15% more than you had planned for the house.

Auctions can be very exciting and dangerous places. Online auctions are safer right? Well maybe, only often you can't see what others are bidding. Some may post all bids on Friday. If no one got the bid, then you can see where everyone else has bid and been rejected. You can raise your bid if you think someone else is bidding. I once won an auction, but it was a painful victory because I was the only bidder and had raised the bid $3000 against myself. You never know on sealed bids, and I had seen someone at the property as I drove by the day before the auction ended and wanted to raise my bid to give me a better chance of getting it. I bought that property for $50,000 with a value of $96,000. Now you understand why I was nervous.

B. You don't get good comps and overpay based on bad research. This you have to be very careful with. Bad research and information can sink you fast. You find a great piece of property with 10 acres and a mobile home on it. Land is going for good money here, and it's under priced. You check, and sure enough, most land in this area is $15,000 to $25,000 an acre. Wow! This deal is really looking good. This land is priced at $10,000 an acre and the mobile home is thrown in for free. Cool! You are going to pick up $50,000 - $100,000 equity on your first deal. Right then you could flip it and surely make $30,000 profit if not more. You have got to get this deal wrapped up before anybody else finds out about it. STOP!

OK, let's take a closer look at the deal. How much road frontage does the property have? Is it sub-divisible? Does it have city water and sewer? Will the mobile home be an asset or a liability? Sure one or two acres lots might be bringing $15-25k an acre, and there may be some sales comps for 10 acres at $200,000, but were they going to be commercial or lakefront or a highway expansion possibility? Is your land a candidate for any of these? Be very careful what you use for comps because you need a real apple-to-apple comparison. Apples to oranges will get you burned.

C. You don't do any research. Well, as you can see from the last example, you won't be any worse off than the guys who are doing bad research, and you will save yourself a lot of time. Never trust other peoples' comps blindly. I've seen a house in one subdivision used as a comp to a house in the subdivision behind it where one had a lot more amenities and much better access.

D. You should always be on your guard against investing too much - too much money or too much emotion - into your real estate investments. Not only are there properties that offer you plenty without requiring that you invest too much of yourself, but investing too much ahead of time almost ensures that you will make costly mistakes.

Run it through the numbers. A basic equation you can use is:

Appraised value or value as repaired minus
The equity position you want minus
Repair costs- whatever is left is your maximum bid,

Example: $100,000   Appraised value as repaired

You want a 25% equity position

- 25,000

Your repair estimates are 10,000

- 10,000

$ 65,000   is you maximum bid or offer

Start lower and make offers until you either get the property or the bid exceeds your maximum offer.

If the bid goes over this price, you let it go. Do not start to rationalize how you could do this yourself or save some money here or there. NO! Do your homework, and if it goes higher than your numbers indicate it is worth to you, let it go. The best way to avoid emotional overinvestment is to do all your investing on paper first. This means calculating how much a property is worth, how much in repairs you need to add, and how much you are willing to pay (tops) for the property. You'll notice that all this information is based on research - there is simply no way you can invest successfully without learning all you can. Knowing what you are doing and how much the property is worth to you dramatically reduces the chances that you will get into a bidding war or will fall in love with a property - both things that ensure you will pay too much.

    * Check your local foreclosure - auction procedures.

2. Getting into a hot market too late.

If a specific market is too inflated due to its reputation as a "hot market", you will end up paying too much. That's not all. If everyone else is investing in a specific market, that demand will boost prices very high - higher than the actual investment is worth. As the ceiling approaches on the market, a panic may occur and people will begin getting out of the hot market, selling out left and right. Anyone who invests in a market when it is hot and sells after its boom generally loses money. In recent times we have seen this in Las Vegas, Detroit, Cape Coral and several other cities. I personally know several investors who suffered major losses as these markets cooled off. Some of them will take years to recover. This is not to say you will always lose money, but it will take very deep pockets to float the property until the market in that area recovers. I have seen people make interest payments for months only to lose the properties eventually anyway. One way to avoid holding the bag in a hot market environment is to get in, make a profit, and get out. Don't hold on waiting to make a killing or you may get killed when the market collapses. Often in preconstruction investments this is not possible, and you may get caught in the collapse.

Unfortunately, it is all too easy to get into a hot market late, simply because of the way that investors often learn about market trends. Far too many investors rely on the news or on professional marketing investment advice in order to figure out what to invest in. Unfortunately, these sources often have outdated or misleading information. Most successful investors do not time the market by listening to where everyone else is investing. They are already investing in markets they researched and are setting the trends of the next hot markets. This is similar to the stock market when the public hears about a great stock and runs in, the smart investors are selling out to them.

You will have much more success if you follow the model of successful investors. Rather than investing where everyone else is investing, figure out what your goals are - are you interested in a steady income, a wealthy retirement, or a lot of profit now? Are you comfortable with risk, or do you want steady, dependable income? Knowing what you are looking for as an investor will reduce the chances that you will simply follow other advisors and investors blindly.

You can also imitate successful investors by looking to where the markets will be hot. Rather than going to the markets that are hot right now, learn to anticipate what sellers, renters, and other investors will be looking for. This is not very difficult if you learn to listen for clues. What do buyers look for? What is lacking in your area right now? What is working for other investors in the country but has not taken off in your area yet? The answers to these questions will often point you in the right direction and let you capitalize before a market gets hot enough to burn you.

For additional, critical real estate mistakes you must avoid and simple solutions to help you avoid these costly errors, go to: www.realestatemistakesyoumustavoid.com

3. Leaving too much on the table.

Often new investors don't ask for enough. Sometimes this is simply because they are afraid to ask, other times it's simply because they don't even think to ask for simple things that can easily add up to cash. Consider what you might ask for:

A. First, you can ask the seller to pay some of your closing costs, for a one-year home warranty, for termite treatment and for a one-year guarantee. Other things you might ask for include appliances, furniture and other equipment. People moving might not need their drapes that won't match at their new home. They likely don't want those blinds that will not fit their new place either. All you need to do is spell it out in your offer or you can include it in an addendum to a counter offer. You can often get the drapes, curtains, blinds, mini-blinds, furniture, appliances, lawn furniture, and other things just by asking. People tend to move these things only to arrive at their new place and realize they moved tons of stuff they really didn't need to move and should have left behind anyway. Educate them. Ask them if they will really need those items. Often they have not stopped to consider leaving them. Ask about where they are moving, maybe it's a very small yard and they won't need that big riding lawnmower. Possibly the new place has all appliances furnished and they won't need those either. They may not need the same items in their retirement home, apartment or new home in Arizona, New Mexico, or wherever they are moving to. Even offering to buy some items from them for pennies on the dollar, you save them plenty of hassle and yourself money and work. Then, you can take the time to sell it yourself. If you will be renting your new home, you can rent it as "partially" (or even "fully") furnished – without spending much on redecorating. If you are reselling, you don't have to pay for house staging. In either case, it's a great deal – all you have to do is ask!

B. Hidden assets. If the house you have just bought has a great spring garden, you may not know it until the spring – unless you ask. Often when properties are bought in the winter you have no idea how beautiful the landscaping is until spring. The local school might have some great programs you aren't aware of but are often of great interest to new tenants or buyers. When buying, be sure to get information about the assets (and hidden assets) from the sellers or last tenants. A simple question like, "What did you really love about this place?" or "What pleasantly surprised you about this place?" or "Are there any great things about this place that are seasonal?" will get you all the information you need about the hidden gems in your new property – and when you show the property to a prospective buyer or tenant, you will know exactly what to point out.

4. Over spending on fix-up and repairs.

If you are investing in real estate, you may have to budget for repairs, fix-ups and clean ups. The simple fact is that many of the best deals in real estate are foreclosure properties and fixer uppers, which may need a little extra work. Being able to buy a home that does not show well simply means that you can buy a home that is under priced and also can mean some sweat equity.

While fixing up may be important, you need to be careful not to overspend. Many beginner investors spend so much on repairs and fix-ups that they end up paying more in renovations and home price than they can get back in profits – and a minus in the profit margin is not what you want!

To avoid this common problem, always do your research up front. Get a professional inspector/contractor to tell you exactly how much money you will need to spend on renovations and repairs and add that total (plus a few thousand dollars in case the repairs go over budget) to the cost of the home. The total cost of the property should be significantly less than what you can get from the property in profits. And don't forget to consider the time of repairs as well as price – properties that require a lot of repairs take time, and may prevent you from a quick resale or carrying costs for 3 months before it is ready to rent.

Once you actually decide to buy real estate that needs help, look for ways to reduce cost. If the property needs paint, for example, look for "oops" paint – paint that is discounted by hardware stores because a buyer goofed on a mixed color. Buy a good quality trashcan with a tight lid to keep your paint in as you mix it. If you are almost finished painting the whole house and you run short on your custom color, don't sweat it. Take a paint stir stick and dip it into the paint and let it dry. Then take the stick to a home improvement store and have them color match it, and then get enough paint to finish the job. Look for sales on items you will use on fixer uppers repeatedly.

Home improvement stores often have light fixtures in multi-packs that are inexpensive. They may also have a ceiling fan sale, up to 20% off. Ceiling fans are a nice upgrade in properties and can also offer an energy savings bonus. Small savings can add up, especially if you put in your own effort into clean up and painting, rather than assigning all the repair work to expensive crews. To finance your repairs, the major home improvement stores often offer 6 months no interest, no payments. If you shop around, you may find them offering the same deal for 12 months. If you find 12 months at one store and you need materials from another, just tell them about the other store's offer and often they will match it. Now, if you know you are going to need to spend a certain amount on repair materials in the next few months, you could purchase gift cards during the 12 month special and use them to make your purchases as you go. You can then make your purchases using your gift cards and not worry about the minimum purchase or if the special has gone off. Now I don't recommend this if you aren't going to use it for your repairs, but it is a very nice way to finance your materials and everybody wins, you save money and the store sells you more materials.

5. Not getting good financing.

If you are investing in real estate, financing can dramatically affect how much of a profit or how good of a deal you can make. Too many investors get so excited by the process of buying real estate that they grab the first financing they can, without really comparing notes. This is a big, costly mistake since large purchases such as properties can really mean huge costs in interest rates. Just by looking for and finding a loan with an interest rate of a percent or two less can mean tens of thousands of dollars in savings. Often by comparing rates and finding a lower one, it can mean savings that really make a property a terrific deal for you.

As an investor, you should know that there are more financing options open to you. You may qualify for a business loan, lines of credit, and partnerships with other investors. You owe it to yourself to check out these options in addition to the more traditional route of mortgages – you may find that alternative means of financing may be more flexible and less expensive in the long run than more traditional property financing.

You should also consider the terms as well as the rates on your financing. If you lock yourself into a long-term loan that is not flexible, you may run into problems when you decide to resell. Make sure that whatever financing you choose that it is flexible enough, as well as cost-effective enough, for your long-term and short-term financial goals.

6. Not having an exit strategy.

Each time you buy a property you must have a plan of how you will get out of this property and what your time frame and cash will allow you to do. This means that when you invest, you need to know:

A. How can this property make me money?

The first step to avoid an emergency down the line begins with your initial purchase. Before buying any property, make sure that you have a realistic plan on how you can make money from the property and realistic plan how much money it will produce. If the housing market goes down, for example, can you rent the property or do something else with it in order to ensure that your money isn't sunk into something that yields no return? Having a plan to make money and finding new ways to make money – such as renting a property week to week as you try to sell – can help ensure that you know exactly what you need to do in order to make money.

B. What is my emergency plan, in case it goes wrong?

A property may have everything going for it, but that does not always mean that it will rent or sell. The market may be bad, a natural disaster may strike – there are many reasons why a property may not be making you money. Before this happens, you better have a good strategy for dealing with the problem. Should you offer the property to a charity for a tax write-off? Should you borrow against the equity until times improve? Should you rent it for a low-ball price? Should you just hold on and wait until the market improves? Plan ahead and come up with several possibilities. Having a few back up plans means that you won't panic and sell off the property for far less than it is worth as soon as times get tough.

7. Getting emotionally attached to a property.

You put blood, sweat, and tears in some of the houses you buy, and so it's no wonder that you just love them. However, it's dangerous to get so attached to your homes that you cannot look at them objectively or offer a good price on them. You may overspend on pampering the home and give up good offers. As an investor, you need to look at properties objectively. If you find yourself getting too involved, step back and do some math on paper. List the assets, drawbacks, costs, and possible profits. Seeing the property as an investment that adds up to neat columns of numbers is a good way to get some perspective. You could also ask a fellow investor what they would do if it was their property, this might prove to be very helpful advice.

Maybe you have fallen in love with this cute little house or great sprawling ranch with a creek and you just have to have it. This is dangerous because it may mean that you end up paying too much for a property just because you like its appearance. The simplest way to avoid this is to make a conscious effort to look for liabilities, as well as advantages, in a property you are considering buying. Get an inspection and assessment so that you have an objective opinion, as well as a good knowledge of any drawbacks of a property.

Getting to know your tenants on a personal level can make evictions very difficult. If you don't evict when necessary, you will watch your money just disappear. There are lots of good reasons to evict: lack of payments, complaints, and even damage to the property. Since no one wants to evict a friend, you need to make sure that your tenants don't become friends. The easiest way to do this without feeling like an ogre is to maintain a professional, friendly relationship with tenants. This means that it's ok to say hello, but dropping by or spending social time with tenants is out. This simple distinction is usually all it takes!

8. Buying investments with a negative cash flow.

Some real estate guru's claim that as long as the negative cash flow doesn't exceed the positive appreciation it is ok to have negative cash flow. Let's think about that for a minute. If you have really deep pockets and are willing to lose plenty of money because the market could slow down, then maybe negative cash flow is not a problem. For the rest of us though, negative cash flow properties are bad news. It's bad enough when you buy positive cash flow properties only to have interest, taxes, maintenance, and insurance chew a hole in your bank account. When you start out with negative cash flow, you are starting behind. This means that you have to work even harder to get into the black and any financial set back could land you heavily in the red.

Experienced investors who can stand to lose money may be able to afford the risks and losses associated with negative cash flow properties, but even they stay away from these properties. With so many real estate investment options, why would you willingly put yourself in a situation that can get you into debt or financial losses over your head? Positive cash flow properties are simply less risky and provide you with at least as many benefits. Negative cash flow real estate, on the other hand, is the one time that additional risk does not necessarily lead to greater payoffs. Unless you really know what you are doing and have a specific plan in mind (not to mention the money in case it all goes wrong) you are better off staying away from negative cash flow.

9. Not verifying the numbers.

There is a saying in journalism: "If your mother tells you she loves you, check it out." Nowhere is the process of fact checking more important than in real estate investing. Unfortunately, plenty of people will tell you partial mistruths or entire whoppers in order to get you to buy – and you are the only one who is responsible for checking the facts and making your decisions based on your own solid research.

If a seller tells you he is getting a specific amount of profit on his property, check it out thoroughly. The seller may be getting homestead exemption or may have a lot better interest rate than you will be getting. The seller may be insured as a homeowner even though it really is an investment property – a risky game that you should never play by the way (if you get caught, good luck with the enormous bills and IRS audits). I bought a commercial property once that, after my closing, I was informed by the county was no longer zoned commercial and would have to be cleaned up. How could this be? Well, the business license hanging on the wall had been paid for with a bad check, thereby losing it the commercial status that was grandfathered in on that property. Several thousand in clean up, rezoning fees and several meetings later, I restored the commercial zoning, but it's amazing how big a mess a bad $35 check can make.

Just because someone has made a specific profit does not mean you will. After all, the seller wants out of the property. They may know something you don't that will affect profitability. Do your research.

When it comes to checking the numbers, by the way, there are several numbers you should be checking. Check the numbers of nearby properties. Find out what other properties in the area draw in profits. Check the assessment value of the property against what is being asked. Check how much you will need to put in yourself for repairs. Check the property taxes, closing costs, possible profits in reselling, and what any liabilities may cost you. Check with the electric company and water department to see what the last 3 years bills have averaged. If you find out the average electric bill is over $500, this might be a problem. If you are renting it out, your tenant may be faced with keeping the lights on or paying his rent. Let me tell you, he will pay the electric bill, and all you will get is the story of his dilemma. Either way, you lose because he can't afford to live there and will move or you will have to evict him. In fact, check and then double-check any numbers, costs, and potential income surrounding a property you are considering buying. It is the single best way to ensure that you have the complete picture before you start putting down your hard-earned money.

10. Not doing a good inspection.

If you are a new investor and don't know much about houses, by all means hire a qualified home inspector. A mistake in assessing a property or estimating repairs could cost you thousands and even ruin your real estate investment career before you get started. Qualified inspectors and assessors aren't just for new investors. Successful, seasoned investors rely on them – and may even hire two to get a second opinion if needed. That's because savvy investors know that a good inspector is your best way of actually evaluating a property.

Inspectors and assessors can tell you whether a property is over priced or on the button and can tell you about potential problems (such as a roof that needs to be replaced or the heat and air unit looks to be on it's last leg) before you buy. An inspection can be a valuable tool in negotiating price and terms because it offers proof of any liabilities in the structure or condition of a property. An inspector can also ensure that you don't get emotionally involved – after all, the job of the inspector is to provide an educated and unbiased view of the property so that you can decide whether the real estate is worth your time and money.

Of course, you will want to hire a good inspector or assessor for the job. Look for someone who is qualified and certified for your area and make sure that you hire someone who has worked in the area for a while. This will ensure that they are aware of local problems and local housing standards. If you are buying in an area that has termites, for example, you want an inspector who has worked in the area long enough to be thoroughly familiar with the signs of pests (and familiar with the ways that sellers try to disguise the damage). Ask other investors and real estate agents in your area who they use. If you have already looked at the property, by all means point out to the inspector areas you are unsure about. Before hiring anyone, make sure that you will get a written statement and report and make sure that the inspector will be looking at all the areas of the property that you consider important.

11. Tenant screening. (Or lack thereof)

12. Paying a fortune for real estate training and not using it.

13. Not looking at enough properties.

14. Always looking for a better deal.

15. Trying to buy from unmotivated sellers.

If some of the examples or stories in this chapter seem farfetched believe me they are not, this is the tip of the iceberg.

Contact information & Additional Resources:

For more information on real estate investing, funding and other related topics you can visit these sites:

www.realestatemistakesyoumustavoid.com
www.letslearnrealestate.com
www.realestatenightmares.com

I hope you have found this helpful and insightful. If you would like to order additional copies of this book or my book *The American Dream - How To Think and Grow Rich*, please go to **www.garywturner.com** or **www.the-americam-dream-how-to-think-and-grow-rich.com**.

Thanks,
Gary W. Turner
Author
Real Estate Investor
Speaker
Motivator

FlippiNq OveR BiG PRofiTs

by FRANK McKINLEY

FROM woRkiNq foR his family's busiNess in a small Northern Arizona town, to traveling around the world in the Navy, to graduating at the top of his class in Beauty School, Frank McKinley has always dreamed of being in business for himself. At the age of 30, he bought a small hair salon in North Scottsdale, AZ, grew it from $70,000 a year in gross revenues to $1 million in just ten years.

Always eager for education and self-improvement, Frank sold his salon in 2001 to start building wealth through real estate investing. His first deal was the purchase of a car wash. Although he planned to purchase the land, the deal went bust and his money was lost. Refusing to give up, Frank turned right back to real estate and ultimately started his own real estate investment company. Through his unique buying and selling techniques, Frank acquired, bought, and sold numerous properties in many states around the country and in just one and a half years, became a real estate millionaire.

As an author of the "Flippin' Explosion," a national trainer and real estate coach for a national real estate educational company. He shared the stage with individuals such as Dr. Dolf de Roos and many other real estate investors. He enjoys helping others pursue their dreams and accomplish their goals. He has presented his techniques to large audiences and has helped many individuals accomplish their dream of making money in real estate through owning and acquiring real estate investment properties. Some of

Frank's students are now real estate millionaires. Real estate investing is his passion and Frank looks forward to sharing his knowledge with as many eager investors as possible!

Flipping Over Big Profits

What is flipping? It's simply buying a house under market value, fixing it up and reselling it in a short amount of time at fair market value for big profits! You go into older run down neighborhoods and revitalize them. Over the years neighborhoods can start to get run down then families start moving out because they can't afford to fix them up themselves. So you can go in and find these great older neighborhoods and start buying run down properties below market value fixing them up and resell them at market value. A lot of times you'll even be turning them over to the some of the same families that moved out of these neighborhoods in the first place because it was getting run down. You see, these families can't afford to fix them up, however they can afford the mortgage payment. A flip unlike a buy and hold strategy, is just getting a property, doing whatever you need to do to fix up that property so you can turn it over to an end buyer. Flipping properties can be a very important and rewarding part of revitalizing your own city and a way for you to give back to your community.

I started fixing and flipping properties because of need: I needed to make money! I wanted to be a real estate investor so without much guidance I bought a business that I thought would get me into the real estate game. I thought that with the cash flow from the business I would eventually be able to purchase the land under it and then go and duplicate this throughout my city and become wealthy in the end. However, it ended up being a very bad deal and I lost all of my life savings on it. That's why I needed money. I didn't quit I got back in the game and started looking for under valued, fixer-upper properties to fix up and resell at a higher a price for a quick profit. It worked!

As a new investor you will go through a natural progression of events you must master in order to find the right deal. Those events consist include: contacting the sellers, evaluating the deal, placing the property under contract, and fixing up and selling the house quickly. If you can't find or purchase houses you are out of business. This book, from starting in this business to getting paid, will explain and sequentially map out for you everything you will need to know. You should be able to recognize what a good deal is and how to proceed for profits. Your profits are based on big discounts. You must let everybody know you're in the business of helping people who need to sell their house quickly.

Your business grows by advertising and marketing yourself, you can place a classified newspaper ad, use the two-foot rule and let everybody know or meet that you are a real estate investor and you are looking for properties to buy. Have a professional looking business card to pass out where ever you go. The more you get out there in the market place the more contacts you will make. Some of those contacts may be other investors or you may even find a wholesaler of properties who you can purchase houses from. You may even find someone less experienced than you are who is willing to have you take them under your wing and train them as a bird dog (someone who scouts neighborhoods for the right houses for you to buy). I personally like to call these people "Property Locators."

Just where do you find the good deals? This is your number one concern. The answer is not that difficult, you just have to look for the clues. Some are obvious and some are hidden just a little bit out of sight. You want the mainstream houses closer to the middle of the city; I've found if you go to the outskirts of town resale becomes more difficult because of fewer buyers and people want to live close to work and conveniences. When you're where most of the people live, you get people that know each other and get referrals from them, you'll sell houses quicker. You want the older houses that are problems 1950's to 1970's, it could be 1900's—1940's (depending on the part of the country your in) that's all you want to look for primarily. These older houses are the ones that work out well. Next, determine the medium house price in your market. Let's say its $200,000, then you will want to find houses $150,000-$250,000 average price range and start looking for motivated sellers in those neighborhoods. You want to find motivated sellers by looking for run down properties, foreclosures in your area, abandoned properties, a job loss, divorce, sickness, death in the family. The best way to find these types of properties is to pass out flyers in the neighborhoods that you are interested in, just target an area and start knocking on doors. For example: look in older neighborhoods, homes that have for rent signs, or appear to have signs that the house is empty, like overgrown yards, no blinds in the windows, piles of newspapers on the front porch. If you find a house that has been vacated knock on the doors of the neighbors houses around that property and ask if they know what's going on with the people of the house you found, do they know their phone number, what time do they usually get home, talk to the mailman, the meter readers; got the idea. Remember, as we stated earlier you go into older run down neighborhoods and revitalize them. The money's where most other people aren't looking. How else would you find these neighborhoods? Drive around and look for dumpsters. Why dumpsters? It's because there are other investors and those investors will help your comparables go up. Once you start going into these neighborhoods and buying these houses, reselling them at a higher price, you actually help your own comparables go up as a result. The next house you flip in that neighborhood could go even a little higher. This will be your bread and butter, it's great and will be your money maker, and it's where you're going to get the best deals and best prices.

How do you determine what a house is worth? If the property cannot be purchased well below market value, there will be no profit in it for you. The numbers have to make sense financially to consider purchasing an investment property. You can work with a local Real Estate Agent but don't spend a lot of time looking at properties already being advertised for sale in your state's Multiple Listing Service. Real Estate Agents have their place but here's why you rarely get a profitable deal from a listed property. A real estate agent is a licensed sales professional; they want to sell houses at full retail price since their commission is directly correlated to obtaining the highest price possible for the seller which is the way it should be. When you are looking to buy a fix and flip property, it is best if you deal with the seller directly. While you are still learning how to evaluate property values in an area, a real estate agent can be a good source of information regarding the property values and activity in an area. You can find a good real estate agent by telling them you are an investor and asking two simple question, "Can you please send me your best deal?" and "Do you invest in real estate?" Then see what they send you. From this statement you can find a real estate agent that you can build a relationship with. Here's why, if they send you a couple dozen properties that are listed on the MLS most likely they don't know anything about real estate investing. If they send you one or two good deals even if they don't work but are reasonably close to what you want you may have found the right real estate agent and they will eventually find a lot of properties for you. If you build a relationship with an agent in your area, use them wisely and treat them fairly.

There are two things you will need to learn about in determining a properties value and they are calculating fair market value (FMV) and comparables. Don't ever assume the seller's asking price is fair market value (FMV). Many sellers and even some real estate agents are unable to accurately value a property. When evaluating properties you must compare apples to apples and oranges to oranges. Apples and Oranges just don't mix when you're determining values. Sellers often believe their home is worth "X" amount of money simply because their neighbor sold their home for "X" amount of money. Is this house in the same shape, square foot and many other determining factors? You will need to learn how to make an accurate assessment and market analysis for a property your thinking could be a deal. In order to determine if a property is a good deal you must have the ability to determine the fair market value (FMV). Realize the asking price or the list price, are not necessarily fair market value but simply what the seller wants. Realize the price could be plucked from the air or a Realtors suggestion of what the house might be worth. This is where comparables are crucial in determining if the subject property is at or below FMV and worth spending any time on. Let's talk about finding the right price for that house, the comparables (comps). Now this can be tricky because are you in a hot market, cooling market or is it a stable market? It changes your comparables because you could pay too much and lose money or try to buy it for to little and lose it to a competitor. I'll start with the basics then describe the different markets next. When you're looking at the comparables it can be all over the board so this isn't time to scrimp on the details. First what is the property square foot that you're looking to purchase? Start looking for houses in that square foot range and maybe 200 square feet of either side of your house. Total all of them up; divide the total of the square feet into the totals of the asking prices you have found. Now you come up with the average dollar per square foot value, then multiple by your square foot and that is your houses average price. Is that the true price? It depends what market you are in. A hot market, cooling market, or is it stable market? If you are in a hot market you may want to use the higher side of your average so not to lose the house to a competitor. If you're in a cooling market use the lower end so it will sell quicker and still make money. In a stable market I would use the average and maybe even slightly lower or so, so you can sell it more quickly. The other things that determines value is bedrooms, bathrooms, lot size, pool, area amenities and of course how the house looks now as to fix up. You can always go to our Web site at www.propertylocatorsite.com to ask the expert for more questions on this.

Comparables are what similar properties have sold for, or what property is selling for in a subdivision or area. To get comparables, drive the neighborhood and call on signs listing houses for sale. You want to get the asking price and the square footage of the house to determine the price per square foot to add to your list and any other pertinent information to determine that it is a similar house you're comparing to. Once you have several properties on your list you can figure out what the average price per foot houses are going for in the area.

Here is an example of how to find the "average price per square foot."

	Price	Sq. Ft.
1204 E. Spruce	$176.500	1324
6701 N. Allen	$193.900	1561
1311 E. Dale	$187.600	1496
1213 E. Camino	$204.700	1735
6674 N. Tucker	$215.500	1800
Total	$978.200	7916
Average = total ÷ by 5 =	$195.640	1583

Average price per square foot $195.640 ÷ 1583= $123.59

Typically in a subdivision, smaller houses will have a higher price per square foot cost than a larger house. By using this formula you will be able to get a good feel for what the fair market value should be on any house in that same area. Obviously if you run across a house in this area priced for $162.500 and the size is 1698 Sq. Ft., that's only $95.70 per Sq. Ft. and at $123.59 per Sq. Ft. its FMV is $209.855 or more. That's a great buy when you realize there's $47.355.00 in equity

What is your profit margin? I always like to start with houses close to 30% or so below market value. It's a good rule of thumb and it has worked well for me. It all depends on several factors. If you want to use this rule of thumb then take a few factors into consideration. First, what's the location? Is it on a busy street, is it near a bad area, across the street from a school etc. I'm looking for anything that may make it stay on the market longer. This may change your asking price. How much fix up is involved? Find a good contractor to give you good ball-park figures, the reason I said ball park is that it can cost more because it there are always unforeseen problems that arise so this also needs to be taken into consideration. What are the average days on market in your area? How much is the money you're borrowing, interest rate and closing cost and this is for buying and selling it. How about the real estate agent commissions when you're selling this house? Take these figures with the fix up cost and maybe an extra 1 – 2% of the house price for those unforeseen problems. This will save you having a headache later, and if you don't use that extra money, you just put more money in your pocket. Now you must decide what you want to resell the home for. Okay, we are taking the fix up cost, average days on market in your area and calculate your holding cost with that number, the interest rate and closing costs for buying and selling it and your real estate agent commissions and add this up then subtract it from your sales price. You now have your starting point other than your profit. How much do you want to make or should you make? I always figure I should get at least 10% of your estimated sales price, so subtract that and now you got your maximum offer you can pay for the house.

EXAMPLE: COST OF SELLING YOUR HOUSE.

Based on a $200,000 (FMV) after repairs purchase price

Real Estate Commission	6% (National Average 5-7%)	$12,000
Buyer's Discount (Discount off asking price)	2% - 5% (National Average 3%)	$6,000
Closing Costs	3% (Varies 2% - 4%)	$6,000
Holding Costs (National Average Gross Marketing Time 3 – 6 mos.)	Loan Payments during Marketing ($1000 X 4)	$4,000
Utilities	($150 X 4)	$600
Repairs	(Fix-up, including inside and out)	$10,000
Insurance	(Vacancy Insurance for 6 mos.)	$600
Marketing Costs Appraisal	(Varies - $350 to $550)	$450
Theft	Budget at least insurance deductible	$500
Taxes	Property Taxes ($1,500 per yr./12 X 4 mos.)	$500
Inspection "Got-ya's"	Repairs (Unforeseen items Buyer requires repaired before closing)	$500

Total Cost to Sell $32,150

Your Profit 10% $20,000

On this example you want to purchase a house that (FMV) after repairs is $200,000 and your total cost from purchase till you reselling it is $32,150, leaving you with a starting price of $167,850. If you are going to make a 10 % profit of $20,000, from there your maximum purchase price or offer is $147,850 of (FMV).

Do not procrastinate now! The earlier you set goals and defined your daily action plan the quicker you will have results which means more money in your pocket! This is a people business; you must love helping people. A vast majority of the distressed sellers you are attempting to contact are just people who have some problems that you may be able to provide a solution for regarding their home. You may be uncomfortable at first, get over it and get out of your comfort zone. Taking action leads to new experiences, new experiences allow you to grow, repetition builds confidence and after a couple of contacts, you will see there can be a lot of satisfaction and fun involved.

Don't work with sellers who are not motivated to sell. Typically FSBO's (For Sale by Owners) properties are being sold for retail. The owner is just trying to obtain top dollar for the property without having to pay a real estate agent's commission. This is not to say a good deal can't be found occasionally, but don't waste too much of your valuable time if you determine the owner is simply trying to maximize his profits. Move on to the next prospect. As a investor take note, because you just read most FSBO's are not motivated sellers, they do however make good practice models for you to perfect your speaking, questioning and listening skills on.

You have worked hard studying and researching the neighborhood where you want to buy, you think you have found the right house to purchase, what do you do next? Now is not the time to falter, worrying about if your calculations are correct or if you may be making a wrong decision. Don't suffer from analysis of paralysis by over analyzing a deal. Remember the saying, if you snooze you lose, many a deal have been lost because another investor came in behind you and placed a contract on the property. Regardless of the reason, when a motivated seller no longer wants a house, they want a solution and relief right now. Create the solution, make an offer and if accepted write the contract. You can find many different versions of a Real Estate Purchase Contract on the internet, at office supply stores, Real Estate Attorney or even the local office of your city's board of realtors. I suggest finding a contract that is simple and easy to read and always keep copies in your vehicle. The simpler the contract is, the less chance you have a scaring your seller. The last thing you want is a distressed owner to see you starting to fill out a scary multiple pages contract which can give them negative thoughts about doing the deal. Don't you be afraid of signing the contract either. When the property is under contract the inspection period begins and you will be able to complete your due diligence on the property. If the property does not pass inspection, the deal can either be re-negotiated or the contract canceled. Either way no additional time has been wasted, or has any money been lost. If the numbers are right, you will purchase the property, if the numbers are off, again, you then either re-negotiate the purchase price, or you just simply cancel the contract with no further action required.

Just get it under contract if you don't the homeowner will shop around if do not have a written contract, and even with a contract the owner may try to shop around. Are you beginning to see why time is of the essence, remember if it's not in writing you have nothing? Verbal agreements mean nothing when it comes to real estate transactions.

You closed on the property what do you do now? The optimal amount of time to fix and flip a property and have it back out in the market and sold is within three to four months. You determine your market that you're in if in fact that is feasible and make adjustments in price, area, and the cosmetic changes you need to make as to what appeals to buyers in your market area. You don't ever want to see your house sit there vacant past six months because your money that you expected to make is starting to get eaten away. A three to four months hold time, fixing it, putting it back on the market and selling it is a pretty short time period. We are talking about quick cash flow; putting the house back on the market and getting the house back out to the retail buyer to put families in them, so you can pay your own family's mortgage. So, let's get to work. First things first, start cleaning! Rent a dumpster. Start getting bids from different contractors for the repairs you want done. Curb appeal is very important, paint the outside if needed and fix up the front yard, that's what people will see first. I'll virtually always paint and carpet the inside. Next the kitchen, it may need just new countertops and maybe throw in some new appliances. The kitchen may not always need new cabinets, maybe just new hardware. I like tile floors for the kitchen and bathrooms, remember the first thing that sells that house will always be the kitchen, then second that master bath. Take some care in this, this can make or break you. Have a keen eye as to what is outdated in the home i.e. faucets, lighting and update those. The total fix up time can normally take two to three weeks, but plan on four because of any unforeseen problems that can arise.

You have to do a great job; however, don't over do it. Don't fall in love with the house; fall in love with the deal (the numbers). Resist the temptation to over fix it. Updating the few things I mentioned can be fairly inexpensive and can be the difference between selling the home quicker and for money. Don't get wild and burn up a lot of cash, remember this is a $200,000 home not a mansion, or pretty soon you'll be on the wrong side of that property's profitability. Remember what's the outcome? You're feeding your family! So if you're not careful, you're going to ruin your family's income and profitability. So keep that in mind and I think everybody will be fine, but just don't fall in love with the house. You can have a tendency to really like it when you're done with the house, there's new carpet and paint and it's just fresh and clean and it smells good again, and you look around and say to yourself, "I could live here." It gives you good feeling of accomplishment when you're able to sell a beautiful home to a happy family.

By now you're probably saying to yourself okay great I know how to find a house to flip, fix it up and even determine the buying price and selling price. But I don't have enough money. Now what do I do? There's a lot more money available than you think. You find a house, lets say 65 to 70 cents on the dollar, don't hesitate for a minute that there may be others out there that would love to loan you the money and make a hefty interest rate on it for letting you do the work because they don't know how to do or want to do it. Believe me when I say there are plenty of people out looking for just that. I know because I have gotten money for homes myself this way. Another option is to take over the home owner's payments, by either by getting a lease option or better, the deed to the property along with a purchase and sale agreement stating you are taking over the payments until you sell it. How about your own home equity line of credit, your credit cards borrow from a family member, your boss, conventional financing, a hard money lender that loans you the money based on the house not your credit. You can always take out a newspaper ad about the house. For example, write an ad that states you have a house worth $250,000 for $165,000 would anyone like to loan you the money to fix it and resell it for a nice interest rate and secured by the deed on the property. Believe me when you find a house at the right price you'll find the money. Get creative. Don't stop now!

How to sell as quickly as possible. Hire a real estate agent first, to get as much exposure as possible by having all the other real estate agents in your area previewing your house for their buyers. Place an ad in your local newspaper for an open house. Put out road signs on major streets and intersections near the house and on all corners directing traffic towards your house. Make sure you stage the property, place a few inexpensive silk plants around the house, towels on the towel racks. I always like to use an apple cinnamon scent for my houses. It smells like apple pie when people walk into the house and it makes them feel at home. Bottom line, price it right. Don't get greedy. If you don't it will take you a lot longer time to sell and you will lose money in the process.

In summary; you just have to find motivated sellers that need to sell in your area, because their house needs work their willing to sell it to you at below fair market value. Use your common sense when fixing it; you should know what a house needs to look like to be move-in ready for a family. Also understand that there are a lot of options for families today, so do a great job on color selection, style and upgrades comparable to other houses at that price range. Start building a list of buyers for future properties you are going to sell. Treat people right, the seller, your real estate agent, contractors, buyers etc... and you'll do fine.

If you set your goals, don't give up and stay determined this is a very profitable business. It's fun to change neighborhoods and put families in properties they wouldn't otherwise buy because they couldn't afford the cost to fix it up.

Contact information & Additional Resources:

If you would like to learn more about Fixing and Flipping Properties please contact me at: **Frank@themckinleycompanies.com**. It would be great to hear from you.

Happy and Prosperous Investing!
See our web-site at **www.propertylocatorsite.com**